Foreword by LILIAN DE FIN
Great-Granddaughter of
SMITH WIGGLESWORTH

WHAT'S THIS
JESUS
THING
ALL ABOUT?

Lynn Russell

What's This Jesus Thing All About?

Cover & Page Design: Ashley Hagan, www.inkwellwriters.com
Editing: Deborah Bailey & Ashley Hagan, www.inkwellwriters.com
Paperback ISBN: 979-8-218-51745-8
eBook ISBN: 979-8-9929728-0-1

For churches and small group discounts, please contact:

www.Jesusthing.com

One day, my friend Dana was walking down a street in Dallas, Texas, when she came upon a teenage girl who was crying. Concerned, she asked the young girl if everything was all right. Immediately the teen began to open up and share her troubles. My friend continued to listen, but there was nothing obvious she could do to help, so she offered to pray with her, saying, "Jesus will help you." And the young girl looked up at her and asked, "Who is Jesus?"

This book is dedicated to anyone who may ask:

WHO IS JESUS?

TABLE OF CONTENTS

FOREWORD

If you are looking for a way to move forward with your life, then this book is for you. Are you asking which way you should go? Keep reading, and you will find the answer. My friend Lynn Russell has written this book entitled *WHAT'S THIS JESUS THING ALL ABOUT?* This book is a positive and clear response to this question that many people are asking in these challenging times we are living in. Many questions will be answered for those seeking the truth.

Lynn reminds us that God Is So Powerful, He Can Do Anything—Anytime. And this is the goal of the book you are about to read—to show how God revealed to Lynn the importance of knowing His Son, Jesus, and how we, the church body of believers, are to prepare for His return.

In this book, Lynn shares many of her God-given dreams. In one such dream, the Lord showed her that we are about to experience another major move of God where many people will come to know Jesus Christ. Smith Wigglesworth also prophesied about the greatest revival this world has ever seen. Get ready, get ready, get ready. During this revival multitudes will be saved, and all of them will need to be discipled.

I believe this book will be used by young believers to mentor other young believers in small groups and even one-on-one. This is one of my favorite promises in God's word.

> *"The Lord replied, 'Listen, I am making a covenant with you in the presence of all your people. I will perform miracles that have never been performed anywhere in all the earth or in any nation. And all the people around you will see the power of the Lord —the awesome power I will display for you. But listen carefully to everything I command you today.'"*
> Exodus 34:10-11, NLT

Lynn exhorts us to walk in obedience to the Word of God. Obedience to the Word of God is the key to living a successful life. My prayer for everyone who reads this book is that you will receive the miracle that you need and that God will use you in these end time days to heal the sick, cast out Devils and raise the dead in Jesus' name. God bless you as you enjoy reading this book and making its truths a part of your Christian walk.

Lilian de Fin
Great-granddaughter of Smith Wigglesworth

ENDORSEMENT

If you want to know who Jesus is and why we should know and believe in Him and accept Him as our Lord and Savior, this is the book you want to read, regardless of whether you are a believer or unbeliever. It is a personal account of author Lynn Russell's quest to know Him for herself.

The Apostle Paul told Christians scattered abroad in various regions of Asia Minor in 1 Peter 3:15 (NASB), *"but sanctify Christ as Lord in your hearts, always being ready to make a defense to everyone who asks you to give an account for the hope that is in you, but with gentleness and respect."*

This book reminded me of the simplicity of what Jesus did for us. He paid the price for our sins. The book will encourage you to move forward with God, to get intimate with the Word of God and to be an effective end-time witness for God. It prepares you for the end-time move of God and encourages you in prayer and fasting. It also encourages you by making you aware that God is powerful and can do anything.

As a Bishop and Pastor for over twenty years, I highly recommend this book for teaching and evangelism at the local church.

Bishop Dr. Raymond Nnolim
Senior Pastor of Jesus Embassy Church, Plano, Texas

FROM THE AUTHOR

Thank you so much for reading my book. I want to tell you first how this book came to be. You see, one night, I had the most amazing dream. Though it was many years ago, I vividly remember it to this day. In this dream, I saw an ornate dining table full of all kinds of beautifully colored foods in the most elaborate banquet feast I had ever seen. To my surprise, I was invited to join in and sit at this exquisite dinner table. I was not expecting this, but I remember being so excited to be invited. Then I woke up.

I did not understand what this dream meant, but from that point on, the Lord began giving me a series of dreams to help me understand this invitation. As the years passed, I began to see God's nature, who He is, and His desire to be with me and have a relationship with me. I am so thankful to God for healing me in so many ways, for forgiving me of all my sins through Jesus, and for helping and guiding me by the Holy Spirit. I came to fully realize the value and impact of having God in my life.

This book, which is a series of action steps, will help you (as it did me) understand this invitation God offers to each of us. This book is, at its core, about the importance of knowing Jesus. Hebrews 12:2, NKJV tells us, " … *let us run with endurance the race that is set before us, looking unto **Jesus, the author and finisher of our faith**, who for the joy that was set before Him endured the cross, despising the shame, and has **sat down at the right hand of the throne of God**.*"

As Jesus is *"the author and finisher of our faith,"* my hope is that you will accept the invitation to follow Jesus. It is Jesus who will take each of us to the Father God, and with that decision, there will be a great celebration in the Kingdom of Heaven.

INTRODUCTION

After the amazing dream of being invited to the banquet feast celebration, I received a dream where I was given a series of phrases. I was awakened from my sleep and immediately wrote down the words I heard in my dream:

- ~ We Have Debt, Jesus Took It Away
- ~ Action Is to Be Taken
- ~ We Take It Before God, and We Obey,
  Giving Us Freedom
- ~ Like Lemons, Demons Try to Sour Everything
- ~ We Help Others Take Their Debt Away
- ~ God Is So Powerful, He Can Do Anything—
  Anything Can Happen with God!

As I began to meditate on these specific words, God continued to give me dreams and showed me certain passages from the Bible to help me understand each of these phrases. Through all of this, I came to see basic Christian concepts in a simpler way and learned the enormous value of knowing Jesus. In John 14:7 (NIV), Jesus tells us, *"If you really know Me, you will know my Father as well. From now on, you do know Him and have seen Him."* When we come to know Jesus, we will know the Father God. Jesus makes the Father God known to us through His words and actions. As we read the words of Jesus in the Holy Bible and see His actions, we come to know God's true nature and of His enormous love for each of us.

The Holy Bible includes the Old Testament and the New Testament—together, a collection of 66 books. The Old Testament gives prophecy of the coming of a Savior, the Messiah —Jesus Christ—all written before His birth. The New Testament records events that occurred just before the birth of Jesus, His ministry while on earth, the acts and letters of His first followers, and the events that are to come. But most importantly, the New Testament speaks of God's desire to have a loving relationship with each of us through His Son, Jesus Christ.

Jesus offers us the opportunity to follow His example and to walk with Him daily. If we choose to follow and abide in Jesus, we will soon have an intimate relationship with Him and know His love and nature (John 17:25-26). This is the ultimate goal—to come to know Jesus. In knowing Him, we will know, love, and want to abide in the Father God.

The next pages you are about to read will show you how the Lord revealed Himself to me through dreams, visions, and Scriptures in the Bible. To understand the dreams and visions in this book more clearly, I have used a variety of Bible translations. Most translations, when referring to God and Jesus, capitalize the pronouns, such as: He, Him, His, Your, Me, My … so we have done the same throughout this book. As well, in some cases, words were added in brackets to Scripture quotations to indicate translation or explanation.

We read in the Bible that God gave many people dreams and visions and the interpretation of dreams to express His will on the Earth. Job 33:14-16 (NKJV) tells us, *"For God may speak in one way, or in another, yet man does not perceive it. In a dream, in a vision of the night, when deep sleep falls upon men, while slumbering on their beds, then **He opens the ears of men, and seals their instruction.**"*

God speaks to people in different ways. He may not speak to you in dreams or visions. If He does not, do not be discouraged. I pray that as you seek God, He will begin to reveal Himself to you in a way that is meaningful to you. His personalized revelation will help you to live a joyful life and draw you into oneness with Him through His Son, Jesus Christ (John 10:27).

Chapter One

WE HAVE DEBT, JESUS TOOK IT AWAY

Years ago, I dreamed of a coming move of God on the earth. In my dream, I saw many miracles; the sick were healed, people were set free and delivered from sickness and disease, and many other mighty works of God occurred. These signs and wonders created in people a desire and hunger for God, and the most hardened of hearts were changed and turned to Him. This coming move of God will be so intense that it will cause people to want to know God and love Him with all their hearts.

Did you know that God, the Creator of the Heavens and Earth, wants a personal relationship with us? Yes, each one of us! When God created man and woman, they were in a close relationship with Him, but sadly, as time passed, they chose to go their own way and became separated from God. This separation caused a barrier. To bring us back into a lasting and loving relationship with Him, God sent His Son, Jesus, to take away that barrier that was causing the separation.

One night while sleeping, I heard these words, "We have debt; (but) Jesus took it away." I had no idea what the Lord was saying to me because I had always thought of debt as financial debt. But after studying my Bible, I realized God was talking about "sin debt." Let's look at what the Bible says about sin debt in the first book of the Bible, Genesis. God created man and woman, Adam and Eve, and they dwelled in the Garden of Eden (Genesis 2:8-14). In this garden, they had everything they needed, but most importantly, they had God in their lives. Adam and Eve were free to do as they pleased; however, God gave them a restriction. God had identified two trees in the middle of the garden: the tree of life and the tree of the knowledge of good and evil. The tree of life, if eaten from, would bring eternal life (Genesis 3:22); and the tree of the knowledge of good and evil, if eaten from, would bring death and separation from God. God instructed Adam:

> *"You are free to eat from any tree in the garden; but you must not eat from the tree of the knowledge of good and evil, for when you eat of it you will surely die."*
> Genesis 2:16-17, NIV

Notice that God was giving Adam the choice: to abide with Him and have eternal life or to be separated from Him and die.

Adam and Eve dwelt in the garden peaceably until one day, the enemy of God, called the Devil or Satan, confronted Eve in the manifest form of a snake. He deceived Eve into eating fruit from the tree of the knowledge of good and evil. Eve ate the forbidden fruit and gave the fruit to Adam. Adam chose to please Eve instead of doing what was pleasing to God, and he ate the fruit that was forbidden. Adam and Eve immediately felt the weight of their actions against God (Genesis 3:7-8). This disobedience to God is called sin.

In its simplest form, sin is to rebel against or disobey God,[1] and as God had warned, it resulted in separation and punishment. This sin burdened Adam and Eve personally, and they were now in debt to God for their disobedience. This is sin debt. Adam and Eve were banished from the Garden of Eden and forced to work the land of Earth for their survival because of their sin debt (Genesis chapters 2-3). Even worse, they would live a life separated from God. As God is holy (sacred, set apart[2]), and sin is unholy (wicked), any amount of unforgiven sin, large or small, will separate us from God's presence. Think of it like trying to mix oil and water. They don't mix! Likewise, God and sin do not mix!

Adam and Eve passed their sinful nature onto their children, as we see in the story of Cain and Abel. Abel put God first in his life and gave an offering pleasing to God. Cain, on the other hand, gave an offering that did not please God, and Cain became very angry when it was not accepted. God asked Cain why he was angry and downcast. *"If you do well, will you not be accepted? And if you do not do well, sin lies at the door. And its desire is for you, but you should rule over it"* (Genesis 4:7, NKJV).

Despite this warning, Cain did not change his ways. He remained angry and ultimately acted out his anger and killed his brother Abel. Because of this, God informed Cain that he was under a curse and *"will be a restless wanderer on the earth"* (Genesis 4:12, NIV). Cain was punished for not obeying God and for putting his own will above the will of God (1 John 3:12).

After many generations, God established strict laws to help His people—the Hebrew people, currently known as the Jewish people—to recognize sin clearly. Some of these laws instructed people on what to wear, eat, touch, etc. These instructions are explained in the books of the Old Testament: Exodus, Numbers, Leviticus, and Deuteronomy. In Exodus 20, God gave Moses, the leader of the Hebrew people, a set of laws called the Ten Commandments. An abbreviated version of the Ten Commandments is:

1. You shall have no other gods before Me.
2. You shall not worship graven images (false gods or idols).
3. You shall not take the name of the Lord thy God in vain.
4. Remember the Sabbath day and keep it holy.
5. Honor your father and your mother.
6. You shall not murder.
7. You shall not commit adultery.
8. You shall not steal.
9. You shall not bear false witness against your neighbor. (Do not lie.)
10. You shall not covet. (Do not be envious or jealous.)

GOD'S LAW HELPED PEOPLE RECOGNIZE SIN

Living under the many laws proved to be very difficult, in fact, impossible. This was God's plan in implementing the laws—to make people conscious of their sins. It was important for the people to recognize sin because sin, any sin, will lead to separation from God and ultimately death (James 1:15). If we look at Bible history, in the Book of Exodus and the Book of Leviticus, rather than having the sinner personally pay for the sin with his own life, God allowed for a substitute—the life of an innocent animal. God was very specific in requiring a death sacrifice of an innocent animal to pay, or atone, for sin. For instance, if someone sinned, a goat or a bull would be killed and sacrificed to pay for that sin. These sacrifices were a temporary substitution and had to be repeated every year. This exchange, or substitution, of a person's sin for the death of an innocent animal would forgive the sin and justify the person before God.

Justification means "made right with God."[3] God instructed the people to follow this process to show them the consequences of sin and that all sin ultimately leads to death.

During this period of ritual animal sacrifices, God promised His people a new way in the future—the New Covenant. He planned to send a perfect sacrifice that would take the place of animal sacrifice and atone for all sin, once and for all. God would send His own Son, Jesus Christ, to be killed and sacrificed on the cross. Jesus would be the perfect and final sacrifice, ending the need for any other sacrifice, and by doing this, He would pay off all sin debt of the entire world (Hebrews 4:15; 1 John 2:2). In 2 Corinthians 5:21 (TLV) it explains, *"He made the One who knew no sin to become a sin offering on our behalf, so that in Him we might become the righteousness of God."*

This second covenant that God promised is described in Hebrews 9:13-15, (NLT):

> *"Under the old system the blood of goats and bulls and the ashes of a young cow could cleanse people's bodies from ritual defilement. Just think how much more the blood of Christ will purify our hearts from deeds that lead to death so that we can worship the living God. For by the power of the eternal Spirit, Christ offered Himself to God as a perfect sacrifice for your sins. That is why **He is the one who mediates the New Covenant between God and people**, so that all who are invited can receive the eternal inheritance God has promised them. For Christ died to set them free from the penalty of the sins they had committed under that first covenant."*

WE HAVE DEBT, BUT JESUS TOOK IT AWAY

We all have sin debt because every one of us has sinned. Like Adam and Eve, we will face punishment and distance from God unless our sin debt is forgiven and taken away. Under this new covenant, Jesus Christ is the only acceptable blood sacrifice God receives to take our sin debt away (John 14:6). Through Jesus Christ, our sins are forgiven so we may be brought into the right relationship with God.

> *"For no one can ever be made right in God's sight by doing what His law commands. For the more we know God's law, the clearer it becomes that we aren't obeying it. But now God has shown us a different way to be right in His sight —not by obeying the law but by the way promised in the Scriptures [passages from the Bible] long ago.*
>
> *We are made right in God's sight when we **trust in Jesus Christ** to take away our sins. And we can all be saved in this same way, no matter who we are or what we have done. For all have sinned; all fall short of God's glorious standard. Yet now God in His gracious kindness declares us not guilty.*
>
> *He has done this through Christ Jesus, who has freed us by taking away our sins. For God sent Jesus to take the punishment for our sins and to satisfy God's anger against us. We are made right with God when we believe that Jesus shed His blood, sacrificing His life for us."*
> Romans 3:20-31, NLT

WHAT DID JESUS DO TO TAKE OUR SIN DEBT AWAY?

Jesus was reared and educated in Hebraic traditions and laws. Around the age of thirty, Jesus began His ministry, which was filled with miracles: turning water into wine, healing the sick, raising the dead to life again, delivering those

6

who were oppressed by the Devil, walking on water, feeding thousands on two occasions, and many other miracles. Read the first four books of the New Testament (Matthew, Mark, Luke, and John) for specific details on the life and ministry of Jesus Christ.

Because of all the good and miraculous things Jesus did on Earth, many people turned to Him for direction and guidance. They could see that God was with Him in all He said and did. For this reason, the Jewish chief priests, elders, and teachers of the law grew envious of Jesus and wanted Him put to death.

Jesus was presented to Pilate, the Roman governor of Judea. The Jewish Assembly made many accusations, telling Pilate that Jesus claimed to be the Christ, a king. Pilate asked Jesus, *"Are you the king of the Jews?"* Jesus replied, *"As you say"* (Luke 23:3, TLV). Pilate announced to the crowd that he saw no basis for a charge against Jesus and sent Jesus to Herod, who had local jurisdiction over Galilee. Herod questioned Jesus, but Jesus was silent. Making fun of Jesus' claim to be a king, *"Herod and his soldiers ridiculed and mocked Him. Dressing Him in an elegant robe, they sent Him back to Pilate"* (Luke 23:11, NIV).

Pilate then presented Jesus to the crowd, but the Jewish leaders had turned the crowd against Jesus, and they persisted in their demand for His death. Fearful a riot would break out, Pilate relented, granting their demand (Luke 23). As the custom of the law permitted, a man named Barabbas, who had been thrown into prison for insurrection and robbery, [and murder according to Luke 23:19], was set free, and Jesus took his punishment—death on a cross (John 18:39-40).

Though Jesus was innocent and was hated without cause (John 15:25), the Jewish chief priests, teachers of the law, elders, and crowd insisted on His death. To appease the crowd, *"Pilate had Jesus flogged with a lead-tipped whip. The soldiers made a crown of long, sharp thorns and put it on His head, and they put a purple robe on Him. Hail! King of the Jews! they mocked, and they hit Him with their fists"* (John 19:1-3, NLT).

Jesus took the punishment for Barabbas, but He also took the punishment for each of us—for the past, present, and future sins of the entire world. The chief priests, elders, teachers of the law, and others were there at that moment in time, but it was my sin debt, your sin debt, and the sin debt of the entire world that Jesus paid off when He suffered and died on the cross (1 Peter 3:18).

Roman soldiers were given the order to crucify Jesus to the death. He was nailed onto a wooden cross or a tree, and while hanging there, those present mocked Jesus: *"He saved others, but He can't save Himself! He's the King of Israel! Let Him come down now from the cross, and we will believe in Him. He trusts in God. Let God rescue Him now if He wants Him, for He said, 'I am the Son of God'"* (Matthew 27:42-43, NIV). God could have rescued Jesus from the hands of these evil people, but Jesus laid His life down to be crucified so that all sin debt would be paid in full.

WHAT MADE JESUS' DEATH SO DIFFERENT FROM OTHERS WHO HAVE DIED?

From the beginning, Jesus had always been in the presence of His Father, God (John 1). But now, the Father God separated Himself from Jesus so that Jesus could take upon Himself all sin for all time. (Remember, God and sin do not mix so Jesus, taking on all sin, would have to be separated from the presence of the Father God.) And now, not only did Jesus endure the physical pain of being tortured to death, but Jesus also felt the pain of being separated from His Father

God. On the cross, He cried out to His Father in his native language, *"My God, My God, why have You forsaken Me?"* (Matthew 27:46, NIV). Jesus became the atoning sacrifice so that our sins would be taken away and we may be brought near to the Father God (Galatians 3:13-14). This is hard to imagine, but this was God's plan. Jesus was the Son of God, and He was sent to Earth to be "the perfect sacrifice" to take away the sins of the entire world (1 John 1:2).

DO WE REALLY NEED JESUS TO BE IN RELATIONSHIP WITH THE FATHER GOD?

One night, I had a dream of vigorously scrubbing a closed umbrella that had been soaked in a dark liquid, almost like grape juice. Standing behind me was a person dressed in religious clothing who kept insisting that the umbrella was not clean enough and that I needed to work harder to make it clean. I was washing and scrubbing the umbrella while explaining that I was trying to make it clean. I opened the umbrella, and instantly the dark, liquid droplets jumped off the umbrella, making it perfectly clean.

The umbrella represented me, and the dark, liquid droplets represented my sins. The person telling me to work harder represented my living under the old law. The law tells us we must work off our sin debt to be forgiven and made clean before God. Likewise, I thought I had to work off my sins to be made clean by God. Because of this, I never felt like my sins were truly forgiven.

It is impossible to work hard enough or be good enough to make ourselves clean or acceptable to God (Galatians 2:16). It is only through Jesus Christ, who took all sin debt away, that we may be forgiven of our sins, made in right standing with God, and brought into relationship with Him.

9

This is why He is called our Savior—He saves us from punishment for our sins. Under the New Covenant, salvation is only attained through Jesus Christ. No other sacrifice is required or accepted by God.

This dream helped me clearly understand that I could open my heart to God through His Son Jesus Christ, like opening an umbrella, and instantly all my sins would be washed away, making me clean and putting me in right standing before God. This dream also visually illustrated to me the difference between the two covenants. Under the Old Covenant, the people had to strictly follow the law to be in right standing with God, thus putting their focus on sin and judgment, which would lead to death (Isaiah 64:6-8). But under the New Covenant, God offers us the opportunity to be forgiven of our sins once and for all so we may be restored and remain in a lasting and loving relationship with Him through His Son, Jesus Christ (Hebrews 10).

THE PROMISE OF A RESURRECTION

But wait! After Jesus satisfied the payment for all sin, God did what no one expected. **God raised Jesus from the dead** (Acts 3:15, Romans 8:11). Jesus knew He would be raised from the dead, and He even told people this would happen, but no one understood what He was talking about. On one occasion, the people demanded a sign that He was the Son of God, and Jesus responded:

> *"An evil and adulterous generation (a generation morally unfaithful to God) seeks and demands a sign; but no sign shall be given to it except the sign of the prophet Jonah. For even as Jonah was three days and*

three nights in the belly of the sea monster, so will the
Son of Man be three days and three nights in the
heart of the earth."
Matthew 12:39-40, AMP

A short time later, Jesus explained to the disciples what this meant. *"He must go to Jerusalem and suffer many things at the hands of the elders, chief priests, and teachers of the law, and that He must be killed and on the third day be raised to life"* (Matthew 16:21, NIV). Many thought the death of Jesus on the cross was the end, but it was not. After He died, Jesus was laid in a tomb. Matthew 28:1-7 (AMP) recounts what happened next.

> *"Now after the Sabbath, near dawn of the first day of the week, Mary of Magdala and the other Mary went to take a look at the tomb. And behold, there was a great earthquake, for an angel of the Lord descended from heaven and came and rolled the boulder back and sat upon it. His appearance was like lightning, and his garments as white as snow. And those keeping guard were so frightened at the sight of him that they were agitated and they trembled and became like dead men. But the angel said to the women, 'Do not be alarmed and frightened, for I know that you are looking for Jesus, Who was crucified. He is not here;* **He has risen**, *as He said (He would do). Come, see the place where He lay. Then go quickly and tell His disciples,* **He has risen from the dead.**'"

This angel of the Lord delivered a powerful message. Angels of the Lord are personal agents, messengers, or helpers of the Lord.[4] In the Old Testament, God told certain people details of things to come. These people were called prophets. They spoke of a coming Savior, the Messiah, whom

God would send to save the world from their sins and bring them close to Him. Jesus fulfilled these prophecies. Some of them included that He would be born in Bethlehem and from the line of King David, grow up in Galilee, be betrayed, crucified, resurrected[5] and He would ascend to Heaven. These are just a few of the many prophecies Jesus fulfilled. Jesus is the Son of God and Savior of the world, sent by God to save all people from the punishment of sin[6] (Galatians 4:4-5).

JESUS HAS RISEN!

Sometime after His resurrection, Jesus met with the disciples in Galilee and delivered the following message: *"All authority (all power of absolute rule) in heaven and on earth has been given to Me"* (Matthew 28:18, AMP). He said this because the enemy of God, the Devil, thought he had victory when he saw Jesus die on the cross and laid in the tomb. He thought Jesus was dead forever, but Romans 4:25 (NIV) records that Jesus *"was delivered over to death for our sins and was raised to life for our justification."* We are justified and made right with God because of what Jesus did. God *"has rescued us from the dominion of darkness and brought us into the kingdom of the Son He loves, in whom we have redemption, the forgiveness of sins"* (Colossians 1:13-14, NIV).

God did all of this to show His love for us through Jesus. Further, Jesus showed us the full extent of His love by laying down His own life willingly and dying on the cross (John 13:1). Through Adam's sin, we were separated from God, but through Jesus Christ, the barrier is removed so that we may be reunited with God.

"But because of His great love for us, God, who is
rich in mercy, made us alive with Christ even when
we were dead in transgressions [sins] ...
it is by grace you have been saved,
through faith [belief in]—and this not from
yourselves, it is the gift of God—"
Ephesians 2:5-8, NIV

THE GIFT OF GOD!

Jesus Christ is God's gift to each of us individually, and this gift is given to us freely. My husband, Jim, had an interesting dream to help easily explain the gift of Jesus being given by grace. In his dream, he was meeting someone at a restaurant, and he couldn't find a parking space, so he slipped his car into one of the spots in valet parking. He did not see the attendant, so he thought he would just pay on his way out of his meeting. But when he came out of the restaurant, his car had been towed! He went back into the restaurant to talk to the owner about his car. The owner instructed that Jim's car be returned to him, and Jim was, of course, very thankful. Notice that Jim *unlawfully* parked his car, so it was rightfully towed. But he *asked* the restaurant owner for *forgiveness,* and the owner gave him back his car without requiring payment. The restaurant owner was extending *grace* to Jim as a free gift, even though he did not deserve it.

God extends the free gift of Jesus Christ to each of us, not because of anything we have or have not done but because of what Jesus did for each of us on the cross. Through our faith [belief] in Jesus Christ, our sins are forgiven, even though we don't deserve it, so we may now stand justified and cleansed of our sins before God. Therefore, we are saved by grace through our faith in Jesus Christ.

13

> *"When people work, their wages are not a gift, but something they have earned.* **But people are counted as righteous, not because of their work, but because of their faith in [belief in] God who forgives sinners.** *David [King David of the Old Testament] also spoke of this when he described the happiness of those who are declared righteous without working for it, 'Oh, what joy for those whose disobedience is forgiven, whose sins are put out of sight.'"*
> Romans 4:4-7, NLT

The free gift of Jesus Christ is offered to each of us. So, what must we do to receive this gift? Paul, a Jewish man who became a follower of Jesus Christ, answers this question:

> *"For it was through reading the Scripture that I came to realize that I could never find God's favor by trying—and failing—to obey the laws. I came to realize that acceptance with God comes by* **believing in Christ**...*the real life I now have within this body is a result of my trusting in the Son of God, who loved me and gave Himself for me. I am not one of those who treats Christ's death as meaningless. For if we could be saved by keeping Jewish laws, then there was no need for Christ to die."*
> Galatians 2:19-21, TLB

Paul clearly states that we cannot be saved from the punishment of our sins by our own effort of trying to follow the law or trying to be good enough. We can only be forgiven of our sin debt by the blood sacrifice of Jesus Christ. In other words:

WE HAVE DEBT, JESUS TOOK IT AWAY

What do we need to do to have our sin debt taken away?

14

[1] Excerpts taken from *The Layman's Bible Dictionary*, ©1997 by George Knight and Rayburn Ray. Used by permission of Barbour Publishing, Inc., page 297.

[2] Taken from *Expository Dictionary of Bible Words* by Lawrence O. Richards Copyright © 1985 by the Zondervan Corporation. Used by permission of HarperCollins Christian Publishing. www.harpercollinschristian.com, page 339.

[3] Knight and Ray, *Layman's*, 176.

[4] Knight and Ray, *Layman's*, 26.

[5] Richards, *Expository*, 506.

[6] Knight and Ray, *Layman's*, 164.

Chapter Two

ACTION IS TO BE TAKEN

God extends His love gift of Jesus freely to all, but it is up to us to respond to His offer so that we may have a mutual, loving, and lasting relationship with Him. As we previously read, God had a relationship with Adam and Eve, and they willfully chose to be separated from Him when they disobeyed. To help people recognize sin, God established laws called the Ten Commandments. But He didn't leave mankind there. He provided a way for man to be forgiven of all sin and redeemed back to Him. God did this by sending His Son, Jesus Christ, to take away the sins of the world. Jesus bore our sins and died on the cross so that we could be brought close to God and have eternal life with Him. What a kind and loving God! So, for this wonderful relationship to get started, we need our sin debt to be taken away, and we need to believe and receive God's Son, Jesus Christ.

JESUS AT THE BEGINNING, THE VERY BEGINNING

*"In the beginning was the Word, and the Word was with God, and the Word was God. He was with God in the beginning... He came to that which was His own, but His own did not receive Him. Yet to all who did receive Him, to those who believed in His name, He gave the right to become children of God— children born not of natural descent, nor of human decision or a husband's will, **but born of God**. The Word became flesh and made His dwelling among us.*

We have seen His glory, the glory of the one and only
Son, who came from the Father,
full of grace and truth."
John 1:1-14, NIV

When I read this Scripture, I struggled to process this concept logically. Then I heard the Lord say, "Out of the mouth of God, the Word came forth." In Genesis, God spoke all of creation into existence. Jesus *"was with God and was God,"* and at the appointed time, God spoke forth from His mouth the Word. By God's Spirit, this **Word** then became a **Seed** in the womb of a young Jewish girl named Mary.

This Seed of God grew in Mary's womb, becoming a baby in human form. This baby was born into the world and named *Yeshua*, Hebrew for Jesus, the Messiah (John 1:17, TLV). Jesus is Who John 1:14 is talking about when it says, *"The Word became flesh and made His dwelling among us."* He was raised by His earthly parents in the ways of the Hebrew people and was trained as a carpenter. His ministry on earth began at about the age of thirty and ended approximately three years later when He was crucified and died on the cross. (The life of Jesus is recorded in the first four books of the New Testament.)

Because Jesus was born of Mary, He called Himself the Son of Man; but He is also God's one and only Son and is also called the Son of God. Each one of us was conceived by a perishable seed, and our human bodies will grow old and die, but Jesus Christ is the imperishable **Seed** of God. When we believe and receive Him, His Seed is birthed in us, and we are *"**born again**, not of perishable seed, but of imperishable [seed],* ***through the living and enduring Word of God"*** (1 Peter 1:23, NIV).

This means that from God's mouth the Word came forth, and when we believe and receive this Word (Jesus), He becomes a Seed within us, and we are now born into the everlasting family in the Kingdom of God. In Him, we are given eternal life and *"an inheritance that can never perish, spoil, or fade—kept in heaven . . . "* (1 Peter 1:3-4, NIV). Read Romans 8:1-16, John 3:3, and John 17:3-9.

Then as Jesus grows within us, we will come to know Him, and through Him know the Father God. Jesus said in John 14:6 (NIV), *"I am the way and the truth and the life. No one comes to the Father except through Me. If you really knew Me, you would know My Father as well. From now on, you do know Him and have seen Him."* The Father God sent His Son to provide a path and show us the Way to having a loving and eternal relationship with Him. God's gift of Jesus Christ is freely given, but as with any gift, this gift must be received. Let's look at the steps required to receive God's gift of Jesus Christ.

WE MUST RECOGNIZE WE NEED JESUS

When Jesus was hanging on the cross, He was between two criminals, also being crucified.

> *"One of the criminals who hung there hurled insults at Him: 'Aren't you the Messiah? Save yourself and us!' But the other criminal rebuked him. 'Don't you fear God?' he said, 'since you are under the same sentence? We are punished justly, for we are getting what our deeds deserve. But this man has done nothing wrong.' Then he said, 'Jesus, remember me when you come into your kingdom.' Jesus answered him, 'Truly I tell you, today you will be with Me in paradise.'"*
> Luke 23:39-43, NIV

19

Both men hanging on the cross were condemned to death, but the one criminal recognized he deserved punishment for his wrongdoing and confessed he was a sinner. What opened his eyes to see he was a sinner? This man recognized that Jesus was the Son of God. He was drawn to Jesus because of His purity which also highlighted his own sin. He boldly asked Jesus to take him with Him—into His kingdom. Jesus answered him, *"Today you shall be with Me in Paradise."*

The other criminal was cynical and unbelieving. He did not recognize Jesus as the Son of God, nor could he see His purity and divinity. But the criminal who recognized Jesus as the Son of God, and recognized his need for Him, spoke out his belief and was instantly forgiven and given eternal life.

GOD REQUIRES ACTION

God required action in the Old Testament Bible when the people of Israel (Hebrew/Jewish people) grew impatient as they were making their way out of Egypt and moving toward the land promised to them by God. Along the way, they began to complain and speak out against God and Moses. This was displeasing to God because it revealed their distrust and unbelief. For their punishment, God sent a plague of poisonous snakes (1 Corinthians 10:9). Many were suffering and dying, so the people asked Moses to ask God to forgive their sins and take away the snakes.

> *"The Lord said to Moses, 'Make a snake and put it up on a pole; anyone who is bitten can look at it and live.' So Moses made a bronze snake and put it up on a pole. Then when anyone was bitten by a snake and looked at the bronze snake, they lived."*
> Numbers 21:8-9, NIV

God could have easily just healed the Israelites, but **He required action on their part for them to live**. The bronze snake itself held no power, but this was God's way of allowing their sins to be forgiven. The people had a choice; they could recognize they had sinned and look at the bronze snake at the top of a pole and live, or they could choose not to follow God's plan for forgiveness, do nothing, and die.

> *"Just as Moses lifted up the snake in the desert, so the Son of Man must be lifted up, that everyone who believes in Him may have eternal life.* **For God so loved the world that He gave His one and only Son, that whoever believes in Him shall not perish but have eternal life.** *For God did not send His Son into the world to condemn the world, but to save the world through Him. Whoever believes in Him is not condemned, but whoever does not believe stands condemned already because he has not believed in the name of God's one and only Son."*
> John 3:14-18, NIV

Notice in the above verse that we stand condemned unless we believe. Without Jesus, we are condemned, but those who choose to believe and receive Jesus Christ will be saved from punishment for their sins and given eternal life. We no longer have a bronze snake to look up to. We now look to Jesus Christ, who was lifted up on the cross and lifted up from the grave so our sins may be forgiven, and we may have eternal life. Jesus promised, *"And I, when I am lifted up from the earth, will draw all people to Myself"* (John 12:32, NIV).

ACKNOWLEDGE WE HAVE SINNED AND ASK TO BE FORGIVEN

God sent a messenger to prepare His people for the coming of His Son, Jesus Christ. This man was named John, the cousin of Jesus, and his message was clear: *"Repent, for the kingdom of heaven is at hand"* (Matthew 4:17, NKJV). John was preparing the people for the coming of Jesus Christ. He did this by encouraging them to confess their sins with a repentant heart and to turn to God.[1] Repentance comes from the Greek word "metanoia," which means "to change one's mind."[2]

Repentance is an important step in drawing near to the Father God, as written in 2 Corinthians 7:10 (NIV): *"Godly sorrow brings repentance that leads to salvation ..."* The Apostle Luke encourages us in Acts 3:19-20 (NIV), *"Repent, then, and turn to God, so that your sins may be wiped out, that times of refreshing may come from the Lord, and that He may send the Christ, who has been appointed for you ..."* Repentance wipes out our sins and clears the path for us to receive Jesus Christ. God still loves us when we sin, but any *unforgiven* sin will distance us from Him (Isaiah 59:2).

> *"He who conceals his sins does not prosper, but whoever confesses and renounces them finds mercy."*
> Proverbs 28:13, NIV

Mercy is to have compassion.[3] God is faithful, and He will be merciful when we confess and renounce our sins. I have a friend who found forgiveness and mercy, and as a result, she received great peace and was brought closer to God. My friend wrote:

"I was always a very controlled person; everything in my life was orderly, but after my children were born, I found it difficult to control my anger. I decided I didn't want to live like this, so I sought counseling from a spirit-filled Christian church that offered personal ministry services.

The session began with prayer, and then we moved right into forgiveness through Jesus Christ and knowing the love of the Father God. As we did this, I felt the overwhelming presence of God's love for me. Then I was brought back to a memory from my early 20s. But rather than looking at the situation as I always had, my eyes were now opened, and I saw that what I had done was sin, and it created a barrier between God and me. I came to truly understand that Jesus paid for all my sins (including this one) on the cross. I told the Lord I was sorry, and I received His forgiveness. Knowing that I was forgiven by God allowed me to forgive myself truly.

I had no idea my anger was related to this sin, but by coming before the Lord and asking for Him to help me in my life, all the anger, all the shame, and my hard heart were lifted from me and taken away and replaced with God's love for me through Jesus Christ. I just encourage anyone to go to God and ask Him to forgive you of any and all sin and deliver you from all the effects of that sin. It was life-changing for me, and it will be life-changing for you, too."

Through Jesus, when we recognize and repent for our sins, we will be forgiven, as 1 John 1:9 (NIV) promises, *"If we confess our sins, He is faithful and just and will forgive us our sins and purify us from all unrighteousness.*" To confess means to admit or acknowledge one's sin.[4] Whether our sins seem too little or too great makes no difference. When examined against the purity of Jesus Christ, we see our need to be cleansed. Because we have all sinned, we all need the cleansing of Jesus Christ, and we get this cleansing through what He did for us on the cross.

Again, it's not about what we have done but what Jesus did for us on the cross. Through Jesus, we are cleansed of our sins and brought near to the Father God.

Jim's grandfather, a WWII veteran, came to live with us near the end of his life. Though his family were believers, he would not receive Jesus. On his deathbed, Jim told Grandpa he wanted him to believe in Jesus so they could be together in Heaven forever. Then, Jim felt impressed to read the book of Matthew out loud to his Grandpa. After the reading, we asked Grandpa to squeeze our hand as a sign that he believed in Jesus and wanted to receive Him into his life. We feel he responded and believe that he received Jesus and that God welcomed him into His Kingdom—even though it was just hours before his passing. God is so good! Again, it's not about the things we have done but what Jesus has done for each of us on the cross.

> "*It was through what His Son did that God cleared a path for everything to come to Him—all things in heaven and on earth—for Christ's death on the cross has made peace with God for all by His blood. This includes you who were once so far away from God ... now as a result Christ has brought you into the very presence of God, and **you are standing there before Him with nothing left against you ...**"*
> Colossians 1:20-22, TLB

Under the New Covenant through Jesus Christ, we may confess our sins to God with a sorrowful heart, and we will be completely forgiven of all our sin debt.

Memories of our past sins may come to mind, but Isaiah 43:25 (AMP) states that once confessed, God does not remember our sins. *"I, only I, am He Who wipes out your transgressions, for My own sake, and I will not remember your sins."* (Transgressions mean trespass or sin.[5]) Another friend was also anguishing over her past, and the Lord told her, "I cast your sins into the sea." Psalm 103:12 (NIV) says, *"As far as the east is from the west, so far has He removed our transgressions from us."* Likewise, Psalm 34:5 (NIV) states, *"Those who look to Him are radiant; their faces are never covered with shame."* (Also read Romans 10:11.) This is what being *"saved by grace through faith"* is all about—we are forgiven, and God remembers our sins NO more. Again, it's not about what we have done but about what Jesus did for us on the cross.

Several years ago, I was talking to a woman who was told by others that she was a bad person, and she came to believe this lie. As we were discussing this, the Lord impressed me to tell her that He was pleased with her because she had chosen His Son. It is that simple; it pleases God that we receive His great gift through believing in His precious Son, Jesus Christ (Hebrews 11:6). Again, it's not about what we have done but what He has done for us. By believing and receiving Jesus, our sin debt is taken away, and we come into a personal relationship with Him and through Him to the Father God. This is why believing in and receiving Jesus Christ is essential and foundational. God knows our hearts and wants us to live free, and that includes freedom from our past. Philippians 3:13-14 (AMP) encourages us by stating we should be, *"Forgetting what lies behind and straining forward to what lies ahead, I press on toward the goal to win [supreme and heavenly] the prize to which God in Christ Jesus is calling us upward."* With this in mind, we can now purposely keep our focus on God and not our past.

A man in Acts 9 had a dramatic conversion to Jesus Christ. His name was Saul, also called Paul (Acts 13:9). He was a great sinner, but then he became a great lover of Jesus. Paul stated:

> *"I count everything as loss compared to the priceless privilege and supreme advantage of knowing Christ Jesus my Lord [and of growing more deeply and thoroughly acquainted with Him—a joy unequaled].*
> *For His sake I have lost everything, and I consider it all garbage, so that I may gain Christ, and may be found in Him [believing and relying on Him], not having any righteousness of my own derived from [my obedience to] the Law and its rituals, but [possessing]* that *[genuine righteousness] which comes through faith in Christ, the righteousness which comes from God on the basis of faith."*
> Philippians 3:8-9, AMP

After I read this, I wondered what gave Paul such passion and hunger for Jesus. The Bible records that Paul had a very unusual personal encounter with Jesus. At this encounter, Paul came to quickly understand that Jesus was the Son of God. Paul came to love Jesus so much that his life was completely changed. He even pondered the thought of which was greater: to leave Earth or stay and tell others about Him. God chose that he would stay, and Paul went on to spend much time in prayer and came to know Him personally as a constant companion. Because of this, he was eager to leave his past behind and focus his time and thoughts on Jesus Christ, following His will and His ways, and telling others about Him.

To help me understand the value of knowing Jesus Christ, the Lord gave me an interesting dream. In this dream, I saw the most beautiful blue, jeweled-stoned necklace lying on a table. Blue represents our receiving revelation,[6] precious stones represent value, and a necklace represents a yoke (around the neck) guiding us as we follow. In my dream, I was shocked to see that people, rather than taking the necklace and putting it on, were throwing these precious jewels into the trashcan. The Lord was showing me that, like the cynical criminal hanging next to Jesus on the cross, there will be people who will not recognize or understand who Jesus is and, therefore, will not believe or receive Him.

The Apostle Peter understood the value of Jesus. One day Jesus asked Peter, *"Who do you say I am?' Simon Peter answered, 'The Christ, the Son of the Living God.'"* (Christ means Messiah, God's Anointed One.[7]) *"Jesus replied, 'Blessed are you, Simon son of Jonah, for this was not **revealed** to you by man, but by my Father in heaven'"* (Matthew 16:15-20, NIV). Peter received revelation from God that Jesus was His Son. The other disciples also received this revelation of Jesus and *knew with certainty* that Jesus was the Christ, the Son of the Living God. This belief in knowing with certainty is faith. And this is how it is with each one of us. Revelation (a revealing from God) puts the Word/Jesus in our hearts and in our hearts the Word/Jesus is made known. This is faith—it's a knowing. Hebrews 11:1 (NIV) describes faith as *"being sure of what we hope for and certain of what we do not see."*

According to Romans 12:3, we have a measure or portion of faith to believe. In Hebrews 4:2 (NIV), the Apostles went out to preach the message of Jesus Christ, but when the people heard the Good News of Jesus Christ, *"The message they heard was of no value to them, because those who heard did not combine it with faith."* These people did not use the small portion of faith they had to believe. We must each decide what we will do when we are given the opportunity to receive Jesus Christ. But we can begin by having an open heart and mind, as in the case of a woman named Lydia in Acts 16:13-14. When she heard about Jesus, her heart was opened to believing, and she received Jesus.

When we repent of our sins, believe, and receive Jesus, we can begin to live our new life in oneness with Him. In a dream, I saw a King at the top of a staircase. Then I recognized who He was—He was Jesus, King Jesus. In the Bible, according to the genealogy of Jesus, He is a direct descendant of King David (Romans 1:3), and therefore Jesus is the rightful heir to the throne as King of Israel (Matthew 1:1-6, 17, NKJV). In Matthew 2:2 (AMP) a wise man asks, *"Where is He who has been born King of the Jews? For we have seen His star in the East and have come to worship Him."* Amazingly, this star guided them to Jesus—Jesus, the King of the Jews.

While on Earth, Jesus operated in a kingly manner, with authority and power (Matthew 4:23). Though many were disappointed because they were expecting a traditional king to rise up, Jesus tried to tell them His kingdom was not of this world. They refused to accept this, and Jesus was rejected and crucified (John 18:36). To their dismay (but profoundly true), above His head hung a plaque that read, *"This is Jesus, the King of the Jews"* (Matthew 27:37 NLT). God raised Jesus from the dead and gave Him the title of *"King of all kings and Lord of all lords"* (Revelation 19:16, NLT). After Jesus' death and resurrection, He ascended to Heaven and will one day return as King to rule for all eternity. *"For a Child is born to us, a Son is given to us. The government will rest on His shoulders. And He will be called: Wonderful Counselor, Mighty God, Everlasting Father, Prince of Peace. His government and its peace will never end. He will rule with fairness and justice from the throne of His ancestor David for all eternity"* (Isaiah 9:6-7, NLT). Jesus is this KING.

Interestingly, in my dream of King Jesus, I was at the top of the staircase with Him. The Apostle Paul states about believers, *"And God raised us up with Christ and seated us with Him in the heavenly realms in Christ Jesus"* (Ephesians 2:6, NIV). Now, from the top of the staircase, Jesus extended His hand to me, and I took it. I started to go down the stairs when He gently tugged me back and said, "No, we will go together." (Read Psalm 73:23.) At His initiative, we walked down the steps in perfect harmony. As we went, our steps became faster and faster, and our feet were in perfect synchronization. Because we were in unity, it all seemed to be with such ease, yet very exciting.

This was a new concept for me because, for my whole life, when I thought of Jesus, I envisioned Him on the cross. But in this dream, He appeared to me as KING. Now, I also see Him as resurrected, holding all power and *"authority in heaven and on the earth"* (Matthew 28:18, NIV).

Psalm 139 speaks of being in unity and states:

> *"Where can I go from your Spirit? Where can I flee from Your presence? If I go up to the heavens, You are there; if I make my bed in the depths, You are there. If I rise on the wings of the dawn, if I settle on the far side of the sea, even there Your hand will guide me,* **Your right hand will hold me fast.** *If I say, 'Surely the darkness will hide me and the light become night around me,' even the darkness will not be dark*

to You; the night will shine like the day, for darkness
is as light to You. For You created my inmost being;
You knit me together in my mother's womb. I praise
You because I am fearfully and wonderfully made;
Your works are wonderful, I know that full well."
Psalm 139:7-14, NIV

When I take the hand of Jesus and walk with Him, I am abiding in Him and with Him, and He will show me the way I am to go and lead me to the Father God. Psalm 16:11 (NKJV) tells us, *"You will show me the path of life; In Your presence is fullness of joy; At Your right hand are pleasures forevermore."* God is so good. He wants us close to Him, and we can be if we believe and receive His Son, Jesus Christ, and walk with Him. God is giving us the opportunity to exchange our sins for His great love gift of Jesus Christ. To some, this deal sounds too good to be true. We give our sins to Him and get forgiveness, righteousness, and a loving relationship with Jesus and the Father God. Yes—the invitation for a loving relationship with Jesus and the Father God is offered to each of us, and it is ours for the taking.

Recall that John, the cousin of Jesus, declared, *"Repent for the Kingdom of God is **at hand.**"* Take the hand of Jesus Christ and repent, believe, and receive Jesus into your heart, and walk out the rest of your life hand in hand with Him. This is exactly what happened to a friend. She was raised with another religious belief but became interested in knowing Jesus. Then one night, as she was sleeping, Jesus appeared to her. In her dream, Jesus was dressed in white and was holding His hand out to her. Jesus Himself was inviting her to take His hand! He was standing in a massive vessel (like a boat), and all her religious gods, who were represented as smaller vessels, sank at His appearance. This dream was so vivid and clear to her that it caused her to open her heart to believing and receiving Jesus as the Christ, the Son of God. Amazingly, she had no fear of converting to the Christian faith because she was eager to embrace an all-powerful yet loving God. If you believe God's Word and would like to receive His free gift of Jesus Christ or would like to reconfirm your faith in Jesus Christ, speak to God from your heart and say this prayer as a guide.

> *Heavenly Father God,*
>
> *I recognize that I need Your love, Your peace, and Your forgiveness. I confess that I have sinned, and I ask that You forgive me. Thank You, Father, for sending Your Son, Jesus Christ, to die on the cross so that I may be forgiven of my sins and brought into a right relationship with You. Lord, I am calling on You now, and I ask that You reveal Jesus to me so that I may know Him and You in a personal way. I believe Jesus is Lord, and I believe in my heart that He died for me on the cross and that He was raised from the dead. I receive Him now so He will live in me and I in Him forevermore. Thank You, Lord, for saving me from the kingdom of darkness and for receiving me into Your glorious Kingdom.*

Now, fully receive His love, grace, and mercy, knowing we are truly and thoroughly forgiven. All our sin debt is taken away. We are no longer guilty; we are justified and made righteous in the eyes of God (Acts 2:21).

CONGRATULATIONS!

You are born into the everlasting family of God (John 1:12)!

31

CELEBRATE BY BEING BAPTIZED

In Acts 16, a jailer was keeping watch over Paul and Silas, apostles of Jesus Christ. In this passage, God supernaturally freed Paul and Silas from prison, and the jailer wanted to know this mighty God of theirs.

> *"'Sirs,* **what must I do to be saved?***' They replied,* ***'Believe in the Lord Jesus and you will be*** *saved, along with everyone in your household.' And they shared the word of the Lord with him and with all who lived in his household. Even at that hour of the night, the jailer cared for them and washed their wounds. Then he and everyone in his household were immediately baptized."*
> Acts 16:30-33, NLT

Upon believing and receiving Jesus Christ, this jailer and his *"household were immediately baptized."* In baptism, the believer in Jesus Christ is washed by water, symbolizing our being fully cleansed of all sin. It is also "a testimony of faith and a pledge to walk in newness of life" with Jesus Christ.[8] The Apostle Peter said, *"And this water symbolized baptism that now saves you also—not the removal of dirt from the body but the pledge of a good conscience toward God. It saves you by the resurrection of Jesus Christ"* (1 Peter 3:21, NIV). Simply, baptism is symbolic of our sins being washed away by God's love through our faith in His Son, Jesus Christ.

I was baptized as an infant, but when I more fully comprehended and understood who Jesus was and my need for Him, I wanted to personally re-commit my life to Jesus Christ for myself. So, I decided to be baptized as an adult. Baptism helped me to realize that I was fully forgiven of all my sins, made clean, and given a fresh start. If you have not, I encourage you to openly celebrate your new life by being baptized (Matthew 28:19, Mark 16:16).

The Apostle Paul said, *"For you were **buried** with Christ when you were baptized. And with Him you were raised to a new life because you trusted the mighty power of God, who raised Christ from the dead"* (Colossians 2:12, NLT). Our sinful past is buried, and we are a new creation in Jesus Christ; as Paul further explains, *"Therefore, if anyone is in Christ, **he is a new creation**; old things have passed away; behold, all things have become new"* (2 Corinthians 5:17, NKJV). In another dream, I was shown the importance of burying our past and living out our life as a new creation in Jesus Christ. In this dream, I saw a man die and fall on the floor. As he was dead and lying on the floor, I saw a new person rise up out of his dead body—but the old dead body was still lying on the ground. Now there were two of them: the new man (**reborn as a new creation in Jesus Christ**) and the old man, dead on the floor. Though this man was a new creation, he began to try to pick up the old, dead man from the ground and carry it around. This was very difficult, and he struggled greatly. This was very sad to see, and I realized that he was not supposed to carry the old, dead self around—but he was supposed to *bury* it! Think about this. He needed to bury his past and live out his life **as a new creation in Jesus Christ**.

This sounds easy, but how do we leave our old, dead self behind and walk in newness of life with Jesus Christ? One morning, I woke up hearing these words, *"Who the Son sets free is free indeed."* These words can be found in John 8:36 (NKJV), *"Therefore if the Son makes you free, you shall be free indeed."* I like

33

the NLT translation, *"So if the Son sets you free, you are truly free."* As we take the hand of King Jesus and walk with Him, we can begin to live out our life to the fullest as a new creation.

The Father God offers us yet another gift to help us live our new life in Jesus Christ—the gift of the Holy Spirit. The Apostle Peter said, *"Each of you must repent of your sins and turn to God, and be baptized in the name of Jesus Christ for the forgiveness of your sins.* **Then you will receive the gift of the Holy Spirit"** (Acts 2:38, NLT).

Who is the Holy Spirit?

---

[1] Knight and Ray, *Layman's*, 271.

[2] Retrieved from: https://www.blueletterbible.org; G3340 - metanoeō - *Strong's Greek Lexicon* (kjv) Blue Letter Bible. Accessed 5 Mar, 2025. https://www.blueletterbible.org/lexicon/g3340/kjv/tr/0-1/

[3] Knight and Ray, *Layman's*, 206.

[4] Knight and Ray, *Layman's*, 74.

[5] H6588 - pesa - *Strong's Hebrew Lexicon* (kjv) Blue Letter Bible Accessed 5 Mar, 2025. https://www.blueletterbible.org/lexicon/h6588/kjv/wlc/0-1/

[6] Ira Milligan, *Understanding the Dreams You Dream* (Shippensburg, PA: Destiny Image Publishers, Inc., 1997), 75.

[7] Knight and Ray, *Layman's*, 70.

[8] Knight and Ray, *Layman's*, 43.

Chapter Three

WE TAKE IT BEFORE GOD AND WE OBEY—GIVING US FREEDOM

Now that we have been forgiven of our sin debt and have chosen to believe and receive Jesus Christ, what is next? I heard the Lord say, "You must consider all of God."

"For there are three that bear witness in heaven: the Father, the Word, and the Holy Spirit; and these three are one."
1 John 5:7, NKJV

God consists of all three:

~God, The Father (Creator)
~God, The Word (Jesus Christ, the Word made flesh)
~God, The Holy Spirit (Our Helper)

The Holy Spirit is one of the three persons of God. In the Old Testament, the Spirit of the Lord came upon various people, such as Samson, David, Isaiah, and others (Judges 14:6), (1 Samuel 16:13), (Isaiah 61:1). When Jesus was on Earth, the Holy Spirit came upon Him as He was baptized by His cousin, John, in the Jordan River. After Jesus' death and resurrection, He ascended to Heaven, and the Holy Spirit came to remain here with us on Earth (Acts 1:1-11). Yes, the Holy Spirit is now available to each of us here on the Earth![1] In John 16:7, Jesus tells us it is to our advantage that He go away so that the Holy Spirit will come. The Apostle Paul wrote to Titus:

> *"God our Savior showed us His kindness and love.*
> *He saved us, not because of the good things we did,*
> *but because of His mercy. He washed away our sins*
> *and gave us a new life through the Holy Spirit.*
> **He generously poured out the Spirit upon us**
> **because of what Jesus Christ our Savior did."**
> Titus 3:4-8, NLT

After accepting Jesus as our Savior, the Holy Spirit empowers us to live out our lives as a new creation—to live as Jesus lived. In Acts 1:8 (NIV), Jesus explains, *"You will receive power when the Holy Spirit comes on you."* As the Spirit of the Lord would come upon others to help and guide them, so will the Spirit of the Lord help and guide us. The Apostle Paul states, *"I pray that out of His glorious riches He may strengthen you with power through His Spirit in your inner being, so that Christ may dwell in your hearts through faith"* (Ephesians 3:16-17a, NIV).

How does the Holy Spirit strengthen us? Jesus explains, *"I will ask the Father, and He will give you another Helper (Comforter, Advocate, Intercessor—Counselor, Strengthener, Standby), to be with you forever—the Spirit of Truth, whom the world cannot receive [and take to its heart] because it does not see Him or know Him, but you know Him because* **He (the Holy Spirit) remains with you continually and will be in you"** (John 14:16-17, AMP). The Spirit of Truth is one of the many aspects of the Holy Spirit. John 14:26, AMP, goes on to say, *"But the Helper (Comforter, Advocate, Intercessor—Counselor, Strengthener, Standby), the Holy Spirit, whom the Father will send in My name [in My place, to represent Me and act on My behalf],* **He will teach you all things. And He will help you remember everything that I have told you."** The Spirit is our constant companion, guiding us into all truth, leading us to a greater revelation of Jesus (John 15:26), and helping us in all aspects of our lives.

The Apostle Luke recounts the dramatic arrival of the Holy Spirit in Acts 2. It happened after the death, resurrection, and ascension of Jesus into Heaven. *"When the day of Pentecost came, they were all together in one place. Suddenly a sound like the blowing of a violent wind came from heaven and filled the whole house where they were sitting. They saw what seemed to be tongues of fire that separated and came to rest on each of them.* **All of them were filled with the Holy Spirit ...**" (Acts 2:1-4, NIV). (Also read Ephesians 1:17 and John 7:38.) From our initial acceptance of Jesus Christ, the Spirit remains with us continually (John 14:17), but there is also an infilling of the Holy Spirit. Just as we need an open heart to receive Jesus, we need to be open to receive the filling of the Holy Spirit. When we choose to allow the Holy Spirit to fill us, He will begin to guide us and direct us, making our lives much easier.

The Lord illustrated the importance of our becoming filled with the Holy Spirit in one of the first dreams I ever remember receiving from Him. In this dream, I was standing by a stream with a friend. She took a closed umbrella and laid it in the stream. I watched as the umbrella began to move very slowly in the stream. My friend picked up the umbrella, opened it, and placed it back in the water again. This time the wind filled the umbrella and carried it briskly down the stream. In my dream, my friend said, "Your life is like this umbrella. The Lord wants you to open yourself up to Him, and He will *fill* you so you can flow down the stream of life." When I awoke, I knew this was a special dream. I believed that if I opened myself up to His Spirit, He would somehow make my life easier. John 3:8 likens the Holy Spirit to the wind. Have you ever noticed the ease with which an eagle soars in the wind? It reaches great heights because the wind lifts the eagle under its wings. Similarly, with the help of the Holy Spirit, we reach heights otherwise unachievable.

> *"But those who wait for the LORD [who expect, look for, and hope in Him] Will gain new strength and renew their power; they will lift up their wings [and rise up close to God] like eagles [rising toward the sun]; they will run and not become weary, they will walk and not grow tired."*
> Isaiah 40:31, AMP

We need to let the Holy Spirit fill us like the wind carrying an open umbrella down a stream, allowing us to fly high like eagles. Our lives will be made much easier when we allow the Holy Spirit to help and direct us.

The Apostle Peter taught us how to begin to live our new life. *"Prepare your minds for action; be self-controlled; set your hope fully on the grace to be given you when Jesus Christ is revealed"* (1 Peter 1:13, NIV). Whether we realize it or not, we need the Holy Spirit's help. Though we no longer have sin debt, we may think wrongly in many ways. Therefore, we must change how we think and what we think about. The Apostle Paul writes in Romans 8:5-6 (NIV):

> *"Those who live according to the flesh have their minds set on what the flesh desires; but those who live in accordance with the Spirit have their minds set on what the Spirit desires. The mind governed by the flesh is death, but* **the mind governed by the Spirit is life and peace.***"*

Paul encourages us to purposely set our minds on the things of the Holy Spirit. *"Do not conform any longer to the pattern* *of this world, but be transformed **by the renewing of your mind.** Then you will be able to test and approve what God's will is—His good, pleasing and perfect will"* (Romans 12:2, NIV).

We can prepare and renew our minds through the Word of God. As discussed in Chapter 2, Jesus is the **living** Word of God. God also spoke forth many other words that were recorded by man to form the **written (living)** Word of God. The written Word of God is the Holy Bible or the Scriptures. Through the Word of God, we learn about Jesus and His actions and gain a greater understanding of God's will and His ways. When we read the Bible, we open ourselves like the umbrella once again, and He fills us with more of Himself. The Bible becomes the living Word in us, lifting our hearts and minds to God.

> *"All Scripture is inspired by God and is useful **to teach us what is true** and to make us realize what is wrong in our lives. It corrects us when we are wrong and teaches us to do what is right. God uses it to prepare and equip His people to do every good work."*
> 2 Timothy 3:16-17, NLT

We must look for the truth to find what is true. We seek God's will and His ways in His Word, the Holy Bible. In my early days with the Lord, I dreamed I was traveling on a road. Along the way, there were signs directing me to my destination. In this dream, the Lord said, "If you don't read the signs along the way, you will be full of confusion and uncertainty, but if you read the signs along the way, you will confidently arrive at your destination." As we study the Bible, we begin to see the signs God has provided in His Word. Then as we continue in it, we develop the confidence to know we are going in the right direction in life. Psalm 119:105 (NLT) states, *"Your word is a lamp to guide my feet and a light for my path."*

I once overheard a conversation with someone who came to realize they needed to accept Jesus Christ and get baptized. As they began to read the Bible, they were amazed at the peace it brought them. Many people are intimidated by the heftiness and complexity of the Bible and wonder where to start. Some recommend beginning in the Book of John because it speaks so plainly of God's love for each of us. Personally, I started in Matthew, reading a chapter a day and asking the Lord to help me understand what I was reading. A good place for anyone to start is the first four books of the New Testament (Matthew, Mark, Luke, and John), which detail Jesus Christ's life, His death on the cross, His resurrection, and His ascension into Heaven. In these four books, we learn the *Word of Truth,* which is the gospel message of salvation through Jesus Christ (Ephesians 1:13).

Reading the Bible may seem overwhelming at first, and you may even wonder if it really applies to you, but stay with it! As we continue, God opens our eyes and minds and will reveal things to us just as He did for the disciples and apostles. After His resurrection, Jesus intermingled with two of the apostles as they were going to Emmaus, and the Apostle Luke wrote: *"Then He opened their minds so they could understand the Scriptures"* (Luke 24:45, NIV). I pray the Lord will do the same for each of us—open our minds thoroughly to the Scriptures, giving us a greater revelation of Him.

The Lord gave me a dream to illustrate the freedom and joy God's Word brings us. In this dream, I was driving with someone I dearly loved. Right before our eyes, a large Bible opened up, and we drove into the black letters of the Bible. Our driving into the letters of the Bible represented our diving into the truths found in the Word of God. We then began to talk, our vision became clear, and we found ourselves in the most beautiful place. I looked over at this person, and she appeared to be floating. Her clothing had turned white, and she held a pink Bible that she clutched in her arms. This person had found a passion for Jesus Christ through the words she found in the Holy Bible and was set free—so free that she appeared to be floating. When I awoke, I was filled with great joy to think of this person I loved dearly so free and happy.

This person had received Jesus Christ in her heart and did as Jesus directed in John 8:31-32 (NKJV): *"If you abide in My word, you are My disciples indeed. And you shall know the truth, and the truth shall make you free."* This is how we prepare our minds for action and take steps toward our freedom: We get into the Word of God (dive into the letters of the Bible as in my dream), so the Word of God will get into us! When we understand the Word of God, knowing that it holds words from the mouth of God to us, we will come to see its value. I am reminded of a dream I had. In my dream, I saw a diamond. It was very reflective and glistened beautifully. As I looked closely into the diamond, I saw a cross. When we study the Word of God, we begin to see that Scripture is like a diamond. Not only will the Scriptures become a precious treasure to us, but they will reveal the many different facets of Jesus that are just waiting to be discovered.

Paul wrote in 1 Thessalonians 2:13 (NIV), *"And we also thank God continually because, when you received the word of God, which you heard from us, you accepted it not as the word of men, but as it actually is, the word of God, which is at work in you who believe."* They didn't just accept the Word of God; they let it *work in them*, which changed their thinking and, therefore, changed their lives.

I thank the Lord that we have the living and written Word available and at work in us to give us guidance and direction. If we read and apply God's Word, it will be the greatest guide to becoming prosperous and successful in the ways of God (Joshua 1:8). We will see how Jesus and many others overcame their adversities by following God's direction. Because the Bible holds God's Words, it is our ultimate source—our manual and inspiration for living God's way. I was once given a shirt that read, "When all else fails, read the instructions ... the Holy Bible."

Unfortunately, I've often been too busy for God and to read His Word. Then one night, I had a dream. In this dream, I was busy, busy, busy, and the Lord said, *"Your busyness means nothing to Me.* **Do not walk in dead men's ways"** (Read Philippians 3:19-20). I was busy with unnecessary duties and self-imposed cares in my life, and as a result, I was not spending time with the Lord nor in His Word. The author of Psalm 119:37-41 (NLT), expresses this same concern and prays, *"**Turn my eyes from worthless things, and give me life through Your word.** ... Renew my life with Your goodness. Lord, give me Your unfailing love, the salvation that You promised me."* We can walk in dead men's ways, which will amount to what this Scripture calls "worthless things," or we can walk with our Lord by the help of the Holy Spirit, which leads to life (Read John 8:12).

This is how we are changed and transformed—through an increasing knowledge and understanding of God that renews our minds (Proverbs 2:6; Psalm 119:130). Martha and Mary, who were sisters, opened their home to Jesus. Mary *"sat at the Lord's feet listening to what He said. But Martha was distracted by all the preparations that had to be made. She came to Him and asked, 'Lord, don't you care that my sister has left me to do the work by myself? Tell her to help me!' 'Martha, Martha,' the Lord answered, 'you are worried and upset about many things, but only one thing is needed. Mary has chosen what is better, and it will not be taken away from her'"* (Luke 10:38-42, NIV). In this passage, Jesus emphasizes the importance of listening to Him. Mary had her mind on Jesus, while Martha, who was busy-busy-busy, was missing out! Jesus explained to Martha that Mary had *"chosen what is better,"* and that was to set her mind on the *"one thing"* that is of most importance—Him.

God Himself confirms this point in Luke 9:35 (NIV) where Peter, John, and James (apostles of Jesus) heard a voice say, *"This is My Son, whom I have chosen; **listen to Him.**"* (We will look at this passage in depth at the end of this Chapter.)

LISTENING FOR THE VOICE OF THE LORD

The voice of the Lord is often described as an *inner voice*. In 1 Kings 19:12 (KJV), this is called a "still, small voice." Before He ascended to Heaven, Jesus tells us in John 16:12-13 (TLV), *"I still have much more to tell you, but you cannot handle it just now. But when the Spirit of truth comes, He will guide you into all the truth. He will not speak on His own, but whatever He hears, He will tell you. And He will declare to you the things that are to come."*

In this Scripture, Jesus states that the Spirit will guide us into all truth and will **speak, tell, and declare** to us things that are to come. A friend of mine heard this inner voice of the Lord, and it changed her life forever. She heard the Lord say, "I will always love you. I love you no matter what." To hear these words from the Lord blessed her tremendously.

Yes, the Holy Spirit will speak to us! He will speak, but we must listen so we can hear Him! I worked in children's ministry for a few years, and it amazed me to see how clearly children could hear the voice of the Lord. I would ask, "How do you hear from God?" The answer was, "You listen!" Like these children, we must set aside distractions to get quiet and listen.

Again, we come to hear the Word of God by focusing on Jesus as Mary did in the above story. We must put our focus on the living Word—Jesus, and the written, living Word—the Holy Bible. When we read/study/pray on the Word of God, we will hear from God, and hearing from God will increase our faith in Jesus Christ. The following Scripture states it this way: *"Faith comes by hearing, and hearing by the word of God"* Romans 10:17 (NKJV). This is so important; the **Word of God** helps us **hear** from God, which will **increase our faith!**

As we prayerfully seek God through His Word, we will grow in our relationship with Him and will begin to hear His voice. In John 10:27 (NKJV), Jesus said, *"My sheep hear My voice, and I know them, and they follow Me."* The voice of God will give us revelation of truth, which means the details of our lives are made clear, giving us specific direction about who God is and what He wants us to do.

In another dream, I was at a party, and a young girl said, **"I just don't get this Jesus thing. What's it all about?"** The Lord dropped the answer in my mind very clearly: "Jesus came that we may have life and have it abundantly, and we are to be *filled* with the Spirit so we may *live in* righteousness, peace, and joy." I knew these words were familiar, so I searched my Bible and found them. Jesus said, *"I have come that they may have life, and that they may have it more abundantly"* (John 10:10b, NKJV). With Jesus, we may have an abundant, full, and exciting life.

The other Scripture that I found was Romans 14:17 (NIV), where the Apostle Paul encourages us, *"For the kingdom*

44

of God is not a matter of eating and drinking, but of righteousness, peace and joy in the Holy Spirit, because anyone who serves Christ in this way is pleasing to God and approved by men." This is God's plan; He wants us to have life in His righteousness so we may live an abundant life. Let's take a closer look at living in His righteousness, peace, and joy.

RIGHTEOUSNESS

As we discussed, we are *"made right in God's sight by faith, we have peace with God because of what Jesus Christ our Lord has done for us"* (Romans 5:1, NLT). Because of the shed blood of Jesus Christ on the cross, our sins are forgiven, and we are given salvation (being saved from paying for our sin debt). Our old identity has passed away in Him, and we are made a new creation in Jesus Christ.

One night, I was thinking about His righteousness and what it really means, and I woke up hearing these words from the Lord, **"This is WHO you are."** (The word WHO was strongly emphasized.) When I received God's gift of Jesus Christ, the old me was buried, and I became a new creation. This is WHO I am now. Recall, *"Therefore, if anyone is in Christ, he is a new creation;* **the old has gone, the new has come. . . .** *God made Him who had no sin to be sin for us, so that in Him we might become the righteousness of God"* (2 Corinthians 5:17-21, NIV).

We are a new creation, and the Holy Spirit helps us to mature in our faith. The Bible illustrates this point by using the example of a seed planted in good soil. When the seed is watered, it grows and will bear much fruit. Likewise, when the Seed, Jesus, enters our hearts by watering with the Word of God, His Seed grows within us, and we begin to mature. In the maturing process, we become increasingly renewed to

God's nature and will bear the fruit of the Spirit. As the Apostle Paul explains:

> *"So I say, live by the Spirit, and you will not gratify the desires of the sinful nature ... But the fruit of the Spirit is love, joy, peace, patience, kindness, goodness, faithfulness, gentleness, and self-control. Against such things there is no law. Those who belong to Christ Jesus have crucified the sinful nature with its passions and desires.* **Since we live by the Spirit, let us keep in step with the Spirit.**"
> Galatians 5:16-23, NIV

Fruit from any tree is only as healthy as the source that feeds it. As we continue in the Word and follow the leading of the Spirit, we are transformed and changed into the very likeness of Jesus. We begin to live the kind of life that displays God's splendor and beauty for all to see. John, the cousin of Jesus, told the Pharisees and Sadducees, *"Produce fruit in keeping with repentance"* (Matthew 3:8, NIV). As we remain and continue in Him, we will grow and will begin to produce fruit that reflects God's nature and will become what Isaiah 61:3b (NKJV) calls *"Trees of righteousness, the planting of the Lord, that He may be glorified."*

If we want more of the fruit of the Spirit operating in our life, we must draw closer to Jesus by spending time with Him in prayer and in the Word of God. Jesus tells us, *"I am the vine; you are the branches. If a man remains in Me and I in him, he will bear much fruit; apart from Me, you can do nothing"* (John 15:5, NIV). As our relationship with Jesus grows, we grow closer to God and find ourselves wanting to abide, follow, and walk in His ways and His perfect will.

Many people receive Jesus and are dramatically changed, but most of us will be transformed step-by-step as we follow the leading of the Holy Spirit. The Apostle Paul directs us to: *"No longer follow our sinful nature but instead follow the Spirit"* (Romans 8:4b, NLT). With our focus on the Word of God and the leading of the Spirit, we begin to shed our old ways of thinking and doing things, and we take on the mind of Christ so we can live as Jesus lived. We do this by living in His righteousness.

Notice, we ARE the righteousness of God in Christ Jesus, and now we need to learn to live in His righteousness. One day the Lord impressed on me that **we live in His righteousness when we choose to live a prayerful and fasted lifestyle**. The Lord further explained that prayer is asking and fasting is obeying. Prayer is *asking God* (making our requests known to God, taking it before God). Fasting is obeying God (obeying the will of God over our own will). When we are in complete obedience to the leading of the Lord, this is true humility.

To live like Jesus, we must choose to prayerfully seek and humbly obey God. When we prayerfully and humbly obey God continuously, we will live a righteous lifestyle. The Apostle Paul wrote to the Romans, ***"You are slaves to the one whom you obey**—whether you are slaves to sin, which leads to death, or to **obedience, which leads to righteousness ..."*** (Romans 6:16b, NIV). Put simply, when we obey as the Lord leads, we live in His righteousness. Paul continues in his letter to the Romans:

> *"Thank God! Once you were slaves of sin, but now you wholeheartedly obey this teaching we have given you. **Now you are free from your slavery to sin, and you have become slaves to righteous living.** Because of the weakness of your human*

nature, I am using the illustration of slavery to help you understand all this.

Previously, you let yourselves be slaves to impurity and lawlessness, which led ever deeper into sin. Now you must give yourselves to be slaves to righteous living so that you will become holy."
Romans 6:17-19, NLT

Our becoming holy is to be set apart for God.[2] Paul wrote to the Ephesians, *"with regard to your former way of life, put off your old self ... and be made new in the attitude of your minds, and put on the new self, created to be like God in **true righteousness and holiness"*** (Ephesians 4:22-24, NIV).

The process of living as a new creation in Jesus Christ is to continue in the Word and to follow the leading of the Holy Spirit. Then as we prayerfully seek the Lord and choose to obey, we will live in His righteousness. This is what Jesus did: He spoke what the Father spoke to Him, and He did what the Father showed Him to do (John 12:49-50). Jesus prayed, and He obeyed.

Let's take a closer look at how we may live in His righteousness—choosing to live a prayerful and fasted lifestyle.

CHOOSE TO BE PRAYERFUL

Part of having a prayerful lifestyle means taking our personal concerns before God in prayer and praying for others. *"Do not be anxious about anything, but in everything, by prayer and petition, with thanksgiving, present your requests to God"* (Philippians 4:6, NIV).

Unfortunately, when you suggest people pray about their life situations, some shrug their shoulders as if to say, "What's the use?" I know because I did this myself. Then one night I had a dream where I was making major decisions without consulting the Lord. As a result, I was miserable. The Lord said to me, "You did not ask Me what I had for you." The Lord was right! This dream made me realize I needed to include God in my life!

God cares so much for us that He will help us with even minor practical matters. Many years ago, we were trying to get my sister into a certain school. Then one night, I had a dream. In the dream, I was asked, "Did you pray about getting into the school?" I began to list all the reasons she should go, and then I was asked *again*, "DID you pray?" At that moment, I realized I had not prayed! So, we prayed, and though there was a waiting list, she got into the school. Through this and other experiences, I came to understand the importance of prayer.

God is faithful; He will answer, but it is our responsibility to ask. James 4:2b (NIV) tells us, "*You do not have, because you do not ask God.*" Some of life's situations may not have quick answers, but Matthew 7:7 encourages us to keep on asking. If we keep on seeking, we will find; keep on knocking and the door will be opened to us. The reason we go to God in prayer is because God has our answer. God's solutions and direction may come to us in various ways, such as through a sermon, vision, or dream, but the primary way we know God's will is through the Word of God and by the revelation of the Holy Spirit (1 Thessalonians 5:21). For example, many years ago, my husband and I were planning to buy our first house together. We found a house we loved, but we were not sure if it was a good purchase, so we prayed. The Lord gave me Deuteronomy 3:18 (NIV), "*The Lord your God has given you this*

49

land to take possession of it." With this Word, we bought the house and enjoyed it for many years.

Acts 2:28 (NIV) is one of my favorite Scriptures. "*You have made known to me the paths of life; You will fill me with joy in your presence.*" It brings great peace and joy to know the will of the Lord so that we may follow it. Many years ago, the Lord told a friend of mine to "*Find the truth and walk in faith.*" My friend prayed she would understand what the Lord was saying to her, but much time passed, and I asked the Lord about this. Then I heard from the Lord. He explained that the Words of God would be "life to those who FIND them." I woke up wondering what this meant and found the answer in Proverbs 4:20-22 (NIV): "*My son, pay attention to what I say;* **listen closely to My words.** *Do not let them out of your sight, keep them within your heart;* **for they are life to those who find them and health to a man's whole body.**"

The Lord was telling my friend to prayerfully go to the Word of God as led by the Holy Spirit in order to find the truth. Recall John 8:31-32 (NKJV): "*If you abide in My word, you are My disciples indeed. And you shall know the truth, and the truth shall make you free.*" Notice, we are to find and come to know THE truth (not our own thoughts and opinions), and God's truth will make us free. We find God's truth in the Word of God (John 17:17), and then we are to obey God's truth by walking it out in faith. The Apostle Paul states, "*The righteous shall live by faith*" (Galatians 3:11, NIV). (Also read: Hebrews 10:38, Romans 1:17.)

Again, it is by prayerfully reading and studying the Word of God that we find the truth. God "*wants all men to be saved and to come to a knowledge of the truth*" (1 Timothy 2:4, NIV). The Word of God is living and powerful (Hebrews 4:12), and it will be alive and active for those who seek and find it. Our part is to get the Word before our eyes, in our ears, and into our hearts, and when we do, it will be life to us. We must always support the "Word" we think we hear by the Word of God—the Bible. This means that if what we hear does not align with the Word of God, it is not from God.

Our answer will be found when we prayerfully seek (personally find God's truth) and obey this truth by faith. To do this, we may need to give up our wants and desires and follow as God leads. And when we obey, we will have a joyous and abundant life. This kind of humble obedience to the Father God's will is a type of fasting.

CHOOSE TO BE FASTED

In the Bible, fasting is described as abstaining from food and/or drink for spiritual purposes, as mentioned in Matthew 6:16-18. It is hard for us to imagine, but Jesus prayed and fasted for forty days. Esther fasted for three days. Daniel fasted from specific food and drink for twenty-one days while seeking the Lord's direction (Daniel 10). There are also examples of focused prayer and fasting in the lives of Moses, David, and Elijah.[3] Also, many Jewish people fast from sunrise to sunset on the Sabbath.

There is, however, more to fasting than just abstaining from food and drink. Another kind of fast is to fast from one's wants and desires and to choose instead to obey God willingly and humbly. Paul wrote, *"I discipline my body like an athlete, training it to do what it should"* (1 Corinthians 9:27, NLT). Paul is talking about training himself to live a righteous lifestyle: to *choose* to live a prayerful (asking) and fasted (obeying) lifestyle.

If we want God's very best for our lives, we must trust Him by taking our situation before Him and choosing to obey. The Lord gave me a great example of this through a simple dream. At this time in my life, I was in a stressful situation, and one night, I dreamt God was handing me a beautifully wrapped present, and He said, "This is My present to you!" But in my dream, I ungratefully threw it aside. I didn't even take time to see what was inside the box. I just wanted what I wanted! I did not realize that God was divinely arranging things for my benefit, which was His present to me.

Then, in my dream, I saw what looked like a burning campfire with smoke rising. I asked the Lord, "What is that?" The Lord answered, "This is to be your sacrifice." The sacrifice God wanted from me was my obedience to His will and His way (Proverbs 21:3). God wanted me to put my trust in Him while He was arranging things on my behalf. True freedom is not living as we choose but living as the Lord leads. God sees all things—He sees what is ahead when we cannot see the future. I needed to trust God and do my part, which was to obey so He could bless me.

Paul understood the importance of obedience and wrote that we should be *"Obeying God with deep reverence, shrinking back from all that might displease Him. For God is at work within you,* **helping you want to obey Him**, *and then helping you do what He wants"* (Philippians 2:12b-13, TLB). Being obedient is sometimes difficult, especially if we're asked to do something we really don't want to do. But God has the Master Plan, and if we trust Him with our situation, listen for His guidance, and obey Him, we will be blessed. *"Trust in the Lord with all your heart; do not depend on your own understanding.* **Seek His will** *in all you do, and He will direct your paths"* (Proverbs 3:5-6, NLT).

On another occasion, my family and I were struggling with some health issues. Then, one night, the Lord told me we needed flavonoids (plant-based foods, deeply colored fruits and vegetables). So, I added a few fruits and vegetables to my diet, but admittedly, I wasn't very consistent or diligent. Then about two years later, I tested a low positive for Anti-Nuclear Antibodies (ANA).

In prayer, I knew I needed to consume MORE flavonoids. To help us along, my family and I began juicing and blending all kinds of fruits and vegetables. (I thought of this as a Daniel Fast of sorts.) It took a lot of work and discipline, but after some time I was re-tested and the bloodwork showed normal. This was a specific Word from the Lord for me, but after making this adjustment, my family and I felt better!

We do not always have the end in sight, but God does! God's Word can be applied to any situation we are facing. When we seek and find His answer, we can trust that God's blessing is on the other side of our obedience.

James 1:22-25b (NIV) explains, *"Do not merely listen to the word, and so deceive yourselves. Do what it says ... but doing it—they will be blessed in what they do."* In Luke 8:21 (AMP), Jesus said, *"My mother and My brothers are these who listen to the word of God and do it."* Jesus also said, ***"Blessed rather are those who hear the word of God and obey it"*** (Luke 11:28, NIV).

GOD BLESSES OBEDIENCE

You may recall that faith is *"being sure of what we hope for and certain of what we do not see"* (Hebrew 11:1, NIV). When we know God's will with certainty, this knowing gives us a desire to obey. Paul explained this when he wrote that obedience comes from faith (Romans 1:5, NIV). God's revelation about our situation will energize our faith to obey. Upon obeying the Lord, true freedom will be found.

In summary:

~ The Word of God helps us to hear from God (by the Spirit)
~ When we hear from God, this increases our faith to obey
~ When we obey, we are set FREE

Our chapter title is: We Take It Before God and We Obey —Giving Us Freedom. When we come to know the will of the Father (through prayer, the Word of God, and the leading of the Holy Spirit) and choose to obey, we live in His righteousness, and this gives us true freedom. God is so good; **He will help us to obey.** Yes, God can speak to us about our situation, and this Word will change our desire to follow and obey Him. For example, years ago, I was asked to do something I really did not want to do. But when I prayed about it, I heard the Lord say, *"I want you to want to do this."* In an instant, God filled my heart with peace and joy for doing it.

PEACE AND JOY

Living in His righteousness (both asking and obeying) will lead to peace and joy. *"The fruit of righteousness will be peace; the effect of righteousness will be quietness and confidence forever"* (Isaiah 32:17, NIV). Again, this kind of peaceful freedom is found when we ask and obey the Father God. It may not always be easy to obey, but Hebrews 12:11 (NIV) promises us, *"No discipline seems pleasant at the time, but painful. Later on, however, it produces a harvest of righteousness and peace for those who have been trained by it.*" This is the benefit of being filled with the Spirit so that we may live an abundant life in righteousness, peace, and joy. And as we continue to live in His righteousness as led by the Holy Spirit, intimacy, oneness, and relationship with Jesus and the Father God will be created.

RECEIVE THE FILLING OF THE HOLY SPIRIT

Just as we received Jesus by faith, we also receive the filling of the Holy Spirit by faith (Galatians 3:14). The Apostle John stated in John 7:38-39 that the Spirit would be given to those who believed in Jesus and that the Spirit will flow through us like streams of living water.

To receive the filling of the Holy Spirit, all we have to do is ask (John 4:10-14)! Jesus explains that even as earthly fathers give good things to their children, *"How much more will your heavenly Father give the Holy Spirit to those who ask Him"* (Luke 11:11b-13, NLT). If you would like to receive the filling of the Holy Spirit, pray this prayer:

> *Heavenly Father God,*
>
> *I believe that Jesus is Your Word made flesh; He is Your Son—the risen Christ. As Jesus paid the full price to make the Holy Spirit available to me, I ask for the filling of the Holy Spirit. Holy Spirit, rise up within me now so I may experience freedom and live in righteousness, peace, and joy here and now on Earth.*
>
> *Amen.*

You may or may not feel anything after you pray this prayer; however, just say, "Thank You, Lord, for the filling of Your Holy Spirit." The Spirit will help us in this life—if we are willing to let Him! With the Spirit, we can enjoy our journey and know we are sealed and marked as God's own, now and for all eternity (Ephesians 4:30). *"God ... set His seal of ownership on us and put His Spirit in our hearts as a deposit, guaranteeing what is to come"* (2 Corinthians 1:21-22, NIV).

KEEPING OUR FOCUS ON WHAT IS TO COME

As mentioned earlier, when Jesus was being baptized, *"The Spirit came down on Jesus and remained on Him."* Before going to the cross, Jesus asked the Father God three times to take away this difficult mission God had given Him. Nevertheless, Jesus submitted His will to His Father's will and chose to obey. Jesus knew He was going to be rejected, beaten, and tortured, but even worse, He knew going to the cross would require separation from His Father God. As painful as it was, it was necessary for Jesus to suffer all these things. Jesus explains, *"Did not the Christ have to suffer these things and then enter His glory"* (Luke 24:26, NIV)?

Let's look at what gave Jesus the strength to obey. Mark 9:2-10 and Luke 9:28-31 recorded that Jesus took Peter, James, and John to a high mount to pray. As Jesus was praying, the appearance of His face changed, and His clothing became dazzling white. Two men, Moses and Elijah, appeared and began talking with Jesus. They were glorious to see. They spoke to Jesus about how He would fulfill God's plan by dying in Jerusalem. Luke 9:32-35 (NKJV) continues, *"But Peter and those with him were heavy with sleep; and when they were fully awake, they saw His glory, and the two men who stood with Him."* Then came *"a cloud and overshadowed them ... and a voice came out of the cloud, 'This is My beloved Son. Hear Him.'"* The Father showed His love for Jesus and gave Him a glimpse of the glory that awaited Him after He fulfilled His mission of dying on the cross. Interestingly, the Bible describes Moses and Elijah as two men who needed affirmation and encouragement themselves. Each asked for God's glory, and both were affirmed and went on to fulfill their mission on Earth (Exodus 33:22-23, 1 Kings 19:11). Through this experience, the Father God did the same for Jesus.

After His resurrection from the dead, Jesus would be reunited with His Father and *"taken up in glory"* (1 Timothy 3:16, AMP) to the heights of Heaven. Hebrews 1:3 (NIV) further tells us, *"The Son is the radiance of God's glory and the exact representation of His being, sustaining all things by His powerful word. After He had provided purification for sins, He sat down at the right hand of the Majesty in Heaven."* This is where Jesus is—in the heights of Heaven with the Father God.

One morning, just as I was waking, I heard the Lord say, "Keep your eyes on the Holy Mountain." The Bible teaches that the Holy Mountain is the Tabernacle or dwelling place of the Father God.

> *"Send out Your **light** and Your **truth**, let them guide me;*
> ***let them bring me to Your Holy Mountain,***
> *to the place where You dwell."*
> Psalm 43:3, NIV

Jesus came to Earth, died on the cross, rose from the dead, and ascended into glory to the heights of Heaven. Now glorified, Jesus sits at the Father's right side on the Holy Mountain in the Kingdom of Heaven. Though God and Jesus are omnipresent, meaning everywhere at the same time, the Holy Mountain is Their heavenly home. To help guide each of us, the Father God will send out His light and truth to draw us to the Holy Mountain.

THE LIGHT

The glory light that shines and radiates so brightly from the Father (Psalm 26:8), with Jesus at His side, guides and leads each of us as we make our way to the Holy Mountain. In Acts 6:10 and Acts 7:54-60 (NIV), the Holy Spirit and the glory light helped Stephen, a Jewish believer in Jesus, boldly preach the truth about Jesus to the Sanhedrin teachers of Hebraic law. The Scriptures say, *"When they heard this [the Word of Truth—the message of Jesus Christ], they were furious and gnashed their teeth at him. But Stephen, full of the Holy Spirit, looked up to heaven and* **saw the glory of God, and Jesus standing at the right hand of God"** (Acts 7:54-55, NIV). Shortly after, Stephen was taken outside the city and stoned to death.

Stephen was full of the Holy Spirit, and his destination was in sight: *"the glory of God, and Jesus standing at the right hand of God."* This glimpse of glory gave Stephen the ability to look past his current circumstance and even forgive those stoning him, stating, *"Lord, do not hold this sin against them"* (Acts 7:60, NIV). As the Father God encouraged Stephen, so will He encourage us as we journey through this life to the Holy Mountain of the Kingdom of Heaven.

There was a man in the crowd who consented to the stoning of Stephen, and his name was Saul of Tarsus. Saul had been attempting to kill all followers of Jesus Christ, until one day while traveling to a city named Damascus, Saul personally encountered Jesus. *"A* **light from heaven** *flashed around him. He fell to the ground and heard a voice say to him, 'Saul, Saul, why do you persecute Me?' 'Who are you, Lord?' Saul asked. 'I am Jesus, whom you are persecuting'"* (Acts 9:3-5, NIV).

Acts 22:11 (NKJV) calls this light from heaven the **"glory."** The glory light was so great, it blinded Saul. God instructed a man named Ananias to go and place his hands on Saul so that he *"may see again and be filled with the Holy Spirit. Immediately, something like scales fell from Saul's eyes, and he could see again. He got up and was baptized"* (Acts 9:17b-18, NIV). Saul, also known as Paul, saw Jesus Christ in the glory light, believed and received Jesus, and became filled with the Holy Spirit. Paul was transformed and forever changed and went on to write much of the New Testament. As Stephen and Paul learned the truth of Jesus Christ, they were able to keep their eyes on the Holy Mountain, and they had the Holy Spirit and the glory of God to help them.

THE TRUTH

The glory light, and The truth (Word and Holy Spirit—the Spirit of Truth) work together to guide us to the Father God with Jesus at His side. To illustrate this, the Lord gave Jim a dream of a series of glass doors lined up in succession. Standing in front of the doors, he could see God at his destination at the very end. Each glass door represented something the Lord wanted him to walk through. As he walked through each door, he thought he had reached his destination, but then he bumped into the next door. It was unseen because the glass was transparent to him. Every time he bumped into a glass door, the Spirit highlighted an area God wanted him to change in his life. He needed to pass through each glass door without shattering the glass (meaning doing things God's way, not his way) while keeping his focus on the destination—***the radiant glory light of the Father God with Jesus at His side***. As each spiritual truth was revealed to Jim, the Holy Spirit helped him to obey and will continue to help him to the end.

Eternal salvation is the most wonderful gift from God, but God desires for us to mature in our faith. As we choose to live in His righteousness, we will receive a continual filling of *"the Holy Spirit, whom God has given to those who obey Him"* (Acts 5:32, NIV). Recall, the Apostle Paul wrote to the Philippians (below is a different translation):

> *"Therefore, my loved ones, just as you have always obeyed—*
> *not only in my presence, but now even more in my absence—*
> *work out your salvation with fear and trembling.*
> ***For the One working in you is God—***
> *both to will and to work for His good pleasure."*
> Philippians 2:12-13, TLV

God works in us as we continue to walk out our faith by allowing the Word of God and the Holy Spirit to help and guide us. But God also gives us a glimpse of His glory to help us and inspire us to finish our journey to the very end where we will hear, *"Well done, good and faithful servant"* (Matthew 25:21, NIV).

To explain this, the Lord gave me an illustration of a sail on a boat. In this vision, I could see the sail fill out forcefully. I began to pray about this vision and one night, I heard these words, ***"We** (people) **go from glory to glory."*** The Apostle Paul speaks of our going from glory to glory in 2 Corinthians 3:18 (NKJV), *"But we all … are being transformed into the same image from glory to glory, just as by the Spirit of the Lord."* I like the NLT version, *"So all of us who have had that veil removed can see and reflect the glory of the Lord. And the Lord—who is the Spirit—makes us more and more like Him as we are changed into his glorious image."*

In this illustration, each one of us is like a sail upon a boat on the high seas, and the wind filling the sail represents the Holy Spirit. When we are filled with the Holy Spirit, we can better navigate the ups and downs of the waves. Even from a far-off distance, at the peak of a wave, we can catch a glimpse of the glory of the Father and Jesus at His side. Upon seeing the radiant glory light beaming from the Holy Mountain, we are filled with His glory and drawn closer and closer to Him. As we go from peak to peak, we are actually going from *glory to glory*. In this, we become more determined to keep our eyes on the Holy Mountain as God's glory fills us, directs us, and energizes us.

As the glory light so brightly shines on us and in us, we begin reflecting the glory of the Lord to others. Jesus said, *"While you have the Light, believe and trust in the Light [have faith in it, hold on to it, rely on it], so that you may become sons of Light [being filled with Light as followers of God]"* (John 12:36a, AMP). This is the goal: to be filled so we may live a life that reflects Jesus (Matthew 5:14-16).

If we choose to follow the (glory) light and the truth (the Word and Spirit), not only will we be changed, renewed, and transformed into the very likeness of Jesus Christ, but we will be guided to our ultimate destination—to the Holy Mountain in His glorious Kingdom. Paul explains, *"... from the beginning, God chose you to be saved through the sanctifying work of the Spirit and belief in the truth. He called you to this through our gospel that you might share in the glory of our Lord Jesus Christ"* (2 Thessalonians 2:13, NIV). As children of God, we have the assurance that at the end of our journey, the Father God and Jesus Christ will be eagerly awaiting each of us, just as They so eagerly awaited Stephen. This will be a glorious day!

Though Stephen was focused on the Father God and Jesus at His side in Heaven, we see that earthly evil forces came against him. These evil forces were influenced by the enemy of God, the Devil. The Devil tries to stop us from

61

getting close to God. But Jesus shows us how to overcome the Devil and these evil forces. Matthew 3 and 4 explain that after Jesus was baptized by His cousin in the Jordan River, the Holy Spirit descended like a dove and came upon Jesus. Jesus then went into the desert for forty days, where he prayed and fasted, and the Devil, called Satan tempted Him. Jesus says to the enemy of God, *"Away with you, Satan! For it is written, 'You shall worship the Lord your God, and Him only you shall serve.' Then the devil left Him, and behold, angels came and ministered to Him"* (Matthew 4:10-11, NKJV).

Who is the Devil?

[1] Bill Johnson, *Hosting the Presence: Unveiling Heaven's Agenda Workbook*, (Shippensburg, PA: Destiny Image Publishers, Inc. 2012), 57.

[2] Knight and Ray, *Layman's*, 141.

[3] Richards. *Expository*, 265.

Chapter Four

LIKE LEMONS, DEMONS TRY TO SOUR EVERYTHING

Who is the Devil and who are his demons? The Devil and his demons are enemies of God, and their mission on Earth is to steal and kill and destroy (John 10:10, NIV). However, a strong foundation in Jesus Christ, the Word of God, and the Holy Spirit helps us implement God's teachings to equip us and protect us against the evil forces of the Devil and his demons. According to the Bible, the Devil was created by God as an angel along with many other angels. Then, one day, the Devil revolted against God (Isaiah 14:12-14), and he and those angels who chose to follow him were cast out of the Holy Mountain. In Ezekiel 28, the Prophet Ezekiel received a message from God regarding a certain king. Although the message is for an earthly king, it also appears to describe the Devil and reads as follows:

> *"You were in Eden, the garden of God. . . . I ordained and anointed you as the mighty angelic guardian. You had access to the holy mountain of God and walked among the stones of fire. You were blameless in all you did from the day you were created until the day evil was found in you. Your rich commerce led you to violence, and you sinned. So I banished you in disgrace from the mountain of God. I expelled you, O mighty guardian, from your place among the stones of fire. Your heart was filled with pride because of all your beauty. Your wisdom was corrupted by your love of splendor. So I threw you to the ground and exposed you to the curious gaze of kings."*
> Ezekiel 28:13-17, NLT

We read in this message for the king a description of the Devil and the explanation for why God threw him out of the Holy Mountain. He was cast to Earth, but his ultimate destination is Hell. Hell is "the place of eternal torment reserved for unbelievers" and is described as a "lake of fire, everlasting destruction, and the second death."[1] God does not dwell in Hell at all; in fact, there is no portion of God in the kingdom of darkness.

As the Holy Mountain is the dwelling place of God, Hell is the ultimate dwelling place for the Devil and his followers. One night, I had a dream of the horrors of Hell. In my dream, I saw what looked like people and/or demons in an open prison. They were bound in black, metal shackles with long chains. The chains were long enough so that they could reach others. I saw what appeared to be three beings fighting each other. I remember two of them biting the third as if they were eating his flesh. He began to cry out in agony and turned his head toward me and looked directly into my eyes. Immediately, I awoke from the dream, sweating and nauseated, with the impression of his face in my mind. In my dream, it was made known to me that there was no hope of escape. This was their life, not only now but forever and ever —eternal damnation.

This dream showed me that the Devil and his demons are evil, and we absolutely do not want to go with them to Hell. Thankfully, God sent Jesus to save us from Hell by taking our sin debt away and giving us eternal life in Him (versus eternal damnation with the Devil). Romans 6:23 (NIV) explains, *"For the wages of sin is death, but the gift of God is eternal life in Christ Jesus our Lord."*

In Luke 10:17-20 (TLV), Jesus sent seventy men to heal the sick and tell people the Kingdom of God is near. The men returned saying, *"Master, even the demons submit to us in Your name!"* Jesus explained, *"I was watching satan fall like lightning from heaven. Behold, I have given you authority to trample upon serpents and scorpions, and over all the power of the enemy; nothing will harm you. Nevertheless, do not rejoice that the spirits submit to you,* ***but rejoice that your names have been written in the heavens.*** *"* Jesus is talking about rejoicing that we have received God's gift through belief in Him so we won't go to Hell. Some people may think they are good enough to not go to Hell, but as discussed in Chapter 1, it is only through Jesus Christ that we are saved from Hell and not of our own doing.

Notice also in the above Scripture that we have been given authority and power over the enemy, that is, the Devil and his demons. If this is so, then why do so many Christians live beaten down and defeated lives? One night the Lord gave me a dream about a certain Christian couple who were living in constant defeat. They appeared to be strong Christians but struggled in many areas of their lives. This confused me, but the Lord gave me another dream to explain what was happening to this couple. In this dream, I saw people coming up out of the center of what looked like a fountain in a round pool. The people coming up out of the water represented all who were baptized because they had believed and received salvation in Jesus Christ. I saw some believers swimming out and others just staying motionless in the center of the pool. Without warning, the Devil suddenly appeared and began touching those who had remained motionless in the water. These people who did not swim out were easy targets for the Devil and his demons. After repeated attacks, they became beaten down and paralyzed in their faith. The Lord was showing me this is what had happened to the

Christian couple in my previous dream who were living in constant defeat.

Conversely, the people who chose to swim out from the center of the pool represented those believers in Jesus Christ who had continued in their faith. Because these believers were moving forward in their faith, they were harder for the Devil and his demons to touch.

> *"So then, just as you received Christ Jesus as Lord,*
> *continue to live your lives in Him, rooted and built up*
> *in Him, strengthened in the faith as you were taught,*
> *and overflowing with thankfulness."*
> Colossians 2:6-7, NIV

Interestingly, a water fountain keeps everything moving. In my dream, it was clear those believers who had chosen Jesus and continued in Him through the Word and with the leading of the Holy Spirit were more difficult for the Devil and his demons to harass and afflict. Deuteronomy 5:33 (NKJV) tells us, *"You shall walk in all the ways which the LORD your God has commanded you, that you may live and that it may be well with you, and that you may prolong your days in the land which you shall possess."* (For further reading, see Deuteronomy 6 and 28.)

While on Earth, God has given us free will to do as we please. *"The highest heavens belong to the Lord, but the earth He has given to man"* (Psalm 115:16, NIV). God wants us to freely choose His Son and freely choose to live in His will and in His ways, but the Devil is allowed time to influence Earth and its inhabitants until God decides to cast the Devil into Hell for all eternity.

THE WORKS OF THE DEVIL ON EARTH

Some people do not believe the Devil and his demons exist, but Scripture informs us the Devil roams Earth where he *"watches everything that is going on"* (Job 1:7 and 2:2, NLT). Several years ago, my sister volunteered at a children's shelter where a child from a highly publicized abuse case was placed. The six-year-old child was given crayons and paper and began to color. She drew a picture of her house and an image of a dark-winged object above her house. My sister asked her what she was drawing, and the child responded, "The angel flying over our house." (Recall that some angels followed the Devil when God cast him out of the Holy Mountain. These angels became demons.) Sadly, this sighting of a dark-winged object reflected the demonic activity going on in this child's home.

Whether we are aware of it or not, we are in a state of war, a spiritual war. As in a worldly war, we prepare prior to going into battle; similarly, we must prepare for this spiritual war. We may take the following action steps to protect ourselves against the Devil and his demons.

~ Understand the works of the enemy
~ Prepare and create your plan according to the Will of God
~ Put on the armor of God

UNDERSTAND THE WORKS OF THE ENEMY

The Devil wants to destroy God's plan for our lives and draw us away from Him. He uses any tactic he can to get us off-track by distracting and discouraging us, and ultimately he wants to steal our hope altogether. The Devil begins in very simple and seemingly harmless ways to make us feel down, bound, and defeated. The Lord gave me an illustration of how the Devil tries to derail us. In this dream, I was shopping, and a woman approached me. "I'll show you some things that are about to be marked down," she said as she led me to the back of the store and out the door. We continued to walk, and then, suddenly, I was standing in front of what looked like the opening of a bottomless mineshaft. I was immediately filled with panic, wondering if the last door had locked behind me. I awoke thinking that the saleswoman represented the temptation of living in a materialistic world where we become so consumed with things that it derails us from our destined path. The bottomless pit represented the hopeless feeling of being in severe financial debt.

The Devil uses such ploys as indulgences to distract us from God's perfect plan for our lives. One night I dreamt of someone trying to drive a car, but he could not reach the pedals. Driving a car represents where we are going in life and not reaching the pedals represents not having control. I looked in the window of his car, and I saw clutter everywhere. Looking in a window represents what is revealed inside.[2] We must be careful not to let time-wasting indulgences such as our phone devices, gaming, social media, shopping, hobbies, and the like get us off-track and ultimately keep us from our destined path.

On a more serious note, the enemy will try to use obsessions, compulsions, and addictions to keep people down, bound, and defeated. Addiction, for example, binds many of us like a slave and can take a variety of forms, like sugar, food, alcohol, nicotine, drugs, and pornography. Any of these things can hinder our walk with Jesus as the Lord showed me in this next dream. In this dream, I watched as a young girl was walking by, and suddenly out of the ground I saw a hand appear and shackle this young girl at the ankle. My eyes were opened to see the Spirit realm. I saw words materialize around her like addiction, sadness, self-criticism, fear, depression, hopelessness, anger, and utter despair. The hand was trying to hold her bound but God wants us to be set free so we can walk with Jesus and live an abundant life in and with Him.

You may be thinking, "Well, I don't have any bad addictions." But the Devil is crafty, and he will tempt us in our own area of weakness. For example, gossip, judgment, or criticism of others may be a weakness for some people, but no matter how seemingly harmless, any sin will distance us from God. *"When tempted, no one should say, 'God is tempting me.' For God cannot be tempted by evil, nor does he tempt anyone; but each person is tempted when they are dragged away by their own evil desire and enticed. Then, after desire has conceived, it gives birth to sin; and sin, when it is full-grown, gives birth to death"* (James 1:13-15, NIV). We must be aware of the enemy's diversions and recognize the Devil's strategy because any sin will draw us away from God.

Under the New Covenant, as we walk with Jesus Christ by prayerfully continuing in the Word of God, God will fill us with the Holy Spirit which helps us break free from the yoke of the Devil. A yoke represents who or what we are bound by. Many of us are yoked to a sinful lifestyle, but Jesus invites us to follow Him: *"Come to Me, all you who are weary and burdened, and I will give you rest. Take My yoke upon you and learn from Me, for I am gentle and humble in heart, and you will find rest for your souls. For My yoke is easy and My burden is light"* (Matthew 11:28-30, NIV).

When we begin to take on the yoke of God through following Jesus Christ, His presence will increase in us, and this will break off the yoke of slavery to the Devil. Therefore, we must willfully purpose to keep our focus on God and walk with Jesus. We can do this by prayerfully spending time in the Word of God and obeying the leading of the Holy Spirit. By doing this, we are strengthened to resist the yoke of the Devil and his demons and free to live the abundant life God has planned (1 Corinthians 9:24).

PREPARE AND CREATE YOUR PLAN ACCORDING TO THE WILL OF GOD

When we have the strategy of the Lord, we are able to protect ourselves from the Devil and his demons. For example, God spared the life of Jesus at an early age because Joseph, the earthly father of Jesus, was warned of an attempt to kill Him. Jesus was the long-awaited King of the Jews, and King Herod was threatened by His arrival. At the birth of Jesus, Joseph was warned by an angel in the night to take Mary and Jesus and flee to Egypt. He was told by the angel, *"Herod is going to search for the child to kill Him"* (Matthew 2:13b, NIV). Thankfully, Joseph obeyed God and took Jesus and Mary to Egypt where they were all protected and kept safe.

Later, when Jesus was grown, Jesus did not act on His own will, but sought and received the Father God's desire and obeyed. Jesus stated, *"I tell you the truth, the Son can do nothing by Himself; He can do only what He sees His Father doing, because whatever the Father does the Son also does. For the Father loves the Son and shows Him all He does"* (John 5:19-20a, NIV). Jesus was humbly obedient to the will of the Father God.

In the book of John, a man named Lazarus became ill and died. Jesus told his disciples that the sickness would not lead to death but that *"... it is for God's glory so that God's Son may be glorified through it"* (John 11:4, NIV). It is interesting for Jesus to say this because Lazarus had already died. But when Jesus got to the gravesite, He *"looked up and said, 'Father, I*

70

thank You that You have heard Me. I knew that You always hear Me, but I said this for the benefit of the people standing here, that they may believe that You sent Me.' When He had said this, Jesus called in a loud voice, 'Lazarus, come out!' The dead man came out" (John 11:41-44a). Everyone saw Lazarus was dead, but God had a different plan. Jesus knew it was God's will that Lazarus would be raised from the dead. Because Jesus knew the Father God's will, He had confidence in God's power to back up His words, and Lazarus rose from the dead.

This process is the same for each of us. We are first to seek and find God's will, and then we can prepare and create our plan accordingly. *"This is the confidence we have in approaching God: that if we ask anything according to His will, He hears us"* (1 John 5:14, NIV). Now that we understand the works of the enemy and have our plan according to God's will, we must put on the spiritual armor of God to protect ourselves against the attacks of the Devil and his demons.

PUT ON THE ARMOR OF GOD

Putting on the armor of God is essential to living a victorious life over the Devil and his demons. The Apostle Paul explains, *"We are human, but we don't wage war with human plans and methods. We use God's mighty weapons, not mere worldly weapons, to knock down the Devil's strongholds."* (2 Corinthians 10:3-4, NLT). A stronghold is defined as "anything on which one relies."[3] I like how a close friend explains a stronghold; it is a series of wrong thoughts that pulls you away from God.

Paul writes a letter to the Ephesians describing the mighty weapons God has provided for us to defend ourselves against the Devil and his demons.

"Finally be strong in the Lord and in His mighty power. Put on the full armor of God so that you can take your stand against the devil's schemes. For our struggle is not against flesh and blood, but against the rulers, against the authorities, against the powers of this dark world and against the spiritual forces of evil in the heavenly realms. Therefore, put on the full armor of God, so that when the day of evil comes, you may be able to stand your ground, and after you have done everything to stand.

Stand firm then, with the belt of truth buckled around your waist, with the breastplate of righteousness in place, and with the feet fitted with the readiness that comes from the gospel of peace. In addition to all this, take up the shield of faith with which you can extinguish all the flaming arrows of the evil one. Take the helmet of salvation and the sword of the Spirit, which is the Word of God. And pray in the Spirit on all occasions with all kinds of prayers and requests. With this in mind, be alert and always keep on praying for all the Lord's people."

Ephesians 6:10-18, NIV

Notice that the Apostle Paul says twice in the above Scripture that we are to *"put on the full armor of God,"* and he also says that we are to *"pray in the Spirit on all occasions with all kinds of prayers and requests."* This means action is required on our part—we must put on the full armor of God. In children's ministry classes, we would act out putting on these pieces of God's armor: the belt of truth, breastplate of righteousness, feet of peace, shield of faith, helmet of salvation, the sword of the Spirit which is the Word of God, and to pray in the Spirit on all occasions. These spiritual Godly weapons are how we effectively protect ourselves from the Devil and his demons. Let's take a closer look at each of these.

72

THE SWORD OF THE SPIRIT: THE WORD OF GOD

Many years ago, my son began to experience repeated injury and illness. I became very concerned and pressed in to seek an answer from the Lord. God revealed to me that through these attacks the Devil was trying to crush his faith. If the Devil can crush our faith, he knows we won't live out our life to the fullest as God intends. In my dream, I was instructed to give my son the Word of God just as you would give water to a very dehydrated person—little by little. Interestingly, Jesus is the living water (John 4). When we take in the Word of God, specifically the words of Jesus, God's Spirit will give life to the Word (John 6:63; John 7:38-39). This would be the same Spirit that raised Jesus from the dead. The Apostle Paul tells us in Romans 8:11 (NKJV), *"But if the Spirit of Him who raised Jesus from the dead dwells in you, He who raised Christ from the dead will also give life to your mortal bodies through His Spirit who dwells in you."*

So, slowly and consistently, I read out loud Scripture verses and stories from the Bible. I also read him other books about God's healing provision for us today, and we watched healing services while continuing to pray. Then one morning, the Lord gave me Psalm 32: *"Surely when the great waters [of trial and distressing times] overflow they will not reach [the spirit in] him"* (Psalm 32:6b, AMP). Through constant watering of the Word of God and prayer, my son was strengthened spiritually and mentally. Then, one day, we were watching one of our healing shows, and the host began to explain that **Jesus' death on the cross was not only for our sins but also for our sicknesses**. Then he began to give a word of knowledge (1 Corinthians 12:8), and my son said, "Come on, Mom, let's pray!" The host said, "There is someone out there who has inflammation of the intestines, and it is very painful for you;

God is healing you right now."[4] With those words, my son felt a tingling in his stomach and said, "I'm healed." The Word of God prepared his heart to receive a touch from God, and he was healed. With this experience, Isaiah 53 came alive to me — Jesus' death on the cross was not only for our sins but also for our sicknesses.

We should hold the Word of God close to us, which is our spiritual weapon, just as the soldiers rebuilding the wall of Jerusalem wore their swords at their side (Nehemiah 4:17-18). The Word of God is called the sword of the Spirit for a reason. When we learn to use the Word of God as a weapon, it will be for us like a sword being wielded against the Devil and his demons.

> *"For the word of God is full of living power.*
> *It is sharper than the sharpest knife, cutting deep*
> *into our innermost thoughts and desires."*
> Hebrews 4:12, NLT

We empower the sword of the Spirit when we get the Word of God in our hearts and minds and proclaim it out of our mouths. The Young's Literal Translation states that the Word of God is the *"sayings of God"* (John 3:34). As cited in Genesis 1, God spoke forth His word and these words formed the sun, moon, stars and all of creation. And God also spoke forth His Word, and this Word was Jesus who came to dwell among us. Many other words were spoken by God and were compiled to form the Word of God, The Holy Bible.

We see Jesus use God's words to protect Himself from the evil one—the Devil. In fact, when Jesus was in the desert for forty days, we are told that the Devil taunted Him. In Luke 4:4 (NKJV), Jesus told the Devil, *"It is written, 'Man shall not live by bread alone, but by every word of God.'"* Jesus was using

God's Word to fight off the temptations and attacks of the Devil, and we should do the same.

One evening, a friend of mine was alone in her apartment where she lived with two roommates. (This is a real-life event, not a dream.) One of the roommates had left the bedroom window open, and a man entered their apartment. Within seconds, the man had a knife to her throat. Immediately, my friend began to quote Scripture! She was able to do this because God's Word was stored up in her—it was imprinted in her mind and engraved upon her heart (Hebrews 8:10). My friend was saying what was in her heart. Whether good or bad, what is stored up in our hearts will come out as Jesus stated, *"Out of the overflow of the heart the mouth speaks"* (Matthew 12:34b, NIV). Although the intruder may not have known what my friend was talking about, he said, "I was going to kill you. I don't know why, but I'm not going to." He actually said this to her and then left!

First John 2:14b (NIV) explains what happened in my friend's situation: *"The word of God lives in you, and you have overcome the evil one."* Because the Word of God was living and dwelling in my friend, she could boldly speak out the Words of God, which not only got her out of a bad situation, but it obviously pierced the heart of the man who broke into her apartment. Knowing the Word of God increases our faith to believe we can call upon the Lord in our time of need. I like the New Living Translation of Ephesians 6:16: *"In every battle you will need faith as your shield to stop the fiery arrows aimed at you by Satan."* In days of old, soldiers would soak their shields in water to extinguish the fiery arrows of their enemy. We, likewise, should soak ourselves in the Word of God, which will give us the ability to extinguish the fiery arrows aimed at us by the Devil and his demons.

THE SHIELD OF FAITH

Early in my relationship with Jim, I dreamt that he had given me a very expensive, huge, eight-foot diamond and ruby red cross. In my dream, we were taking the cross home in our car. Then, a lion began to run after us, and as he was running, he changed into a man. This man stopped our car with his bare hands and took the cross out of the back of our car. The man then said, "Fight me for it." Jim said, "NO, take it." Then I heard the Lord say, "At some point in your lives, Jim and you must make a choice for the real Christ."

God revealed to me that the dream represented a temptation of riches to see which was greater—a love for money or our love for Him. The Apostle Paul wrote:

> *"Command those who are rich in this present world not to be arrogant nor to put their hope in wealth, which is so uncertain, but to put their hope in God ...."*
> 1 Timothy 6:17, NIV

In 1 Peter 5:2b, the Apostle Peter tells us not to be greedy for money. And then he goes on to say: *"Cast all your anxiety on Him because He cares for you. Be self-controlled and alert.* **Your enemy the devil prowls around like a roaring lion looking for someone to devour.** *Resist him, standing firm in the faith"* (1 Peter 5:7-9a, NIV).

The enemy is out there lurking around like a lion, so we must stand firm on the foundation of our faith, Jesus Christ. Isaiah from the Bible stated, *"If you do not stand firm in your faith, you will not stand at all"* (Isaiah 7:9b, NIV). Being well-established in Jesus Christ allows us to stand firm in our faith so that we may resist temptation and the attacks of the Devil and his demons.

One night I had a very odd dream. In this dream, I saw a green, slimy substance under the legs of a bathtub. The bathtub represented me, and the green, slimy substance under my legs was making me unstable. The slime represented a lie, specifically, a distortion of a fundamental truth I had come to believe. This dream was God's way of showing me I had taken on an untrue belief, and He wanted this wrong thinking cleaned out, hence the bathtub! I realized I needed to know for myself what was true according to the Word of God.

THE BELT OF TRUTH

Recall, the Word of God and the Holy Spirit guide us into ALL Truth. As Christians, God wants the foundation of our faith to be accurate and based firmly on the Rock—Jesus Christ, the Messiah, the Son of the Living God (Matthew 16:18). Shortly after this dream of the bathtub, I was given another dream where I was told, "Put God first in your life and spend more time with the Lord." With an eagerness to know the truth, I began to spend time in the Word of God and pray more—making God the priority in my life. Over the next few months, the Lord revealed more of Himself to me, and I began to see the truth which created in me a strong foundation in Jesus Christ.

In order to safeguard ourselves, we can do as the Bereans did. The Bereans, who were of noble character, examined the Scriptures to see if Jesus did, in fact, fulfill the prophecies. They *"received the message with great eagerness and examined the Scriptures every day to see if what Paul said was true"* (Acts 17:11, NIV). If we continue in the Word (Bible), the Holy Spirit helps us to understand and know the truth, and will guide us into all Truth. Without the Word of God and the revelation of the Holy Spirit, we are left to rely on our own thoughts and feelings and therefore are limited in our thinking. But God tells us, *"My thoughts are not your thoughts, neither are your ways My ways"* (Isaiah 55:8, NIV). Though we may not realize it, our own feelings, emotions, and self-limited thinking can mislead and deceive us.

I had a very disturbing dream to illustrate how the Devil tries to mislead and deceive us. In this dream, I saw people meeting in a home. As I walked into the home, I could see some people lying on the floor and others were putting something to their heads which was causing them to die. One man said he was "honored to die for this." I began to ask, "Die for what? He's honored to die for what?" But no one would answer me. It appeared they were holding a gun to their heads, but in looking closer, I realized that it was not a gun. These people were allowing themselves to be brainwashed and therefore came to follow a path that was causing them to die.

> *"There is a way that seems right to a man,*
> *but in the end it leads to death."*
> Proverbs 16:25, NIV

These people were deceived into thinking they were doing something honorable, and they were willing to die for a cause they didn't know or understand. Many people are looking for meaning and truth in life, but unfortunately, they have become deceived and are tricked by the Devil. The Apostle Paul in 2 Corinthians 11:14 (NIV) warns us, *"Satan himself masquerades as an angel of light."*

The Apostle John wrote that the Devil *"was a murderer from the beginning and has always hated the truth. There is no truth in him. When he lies, it is consistent with his character; for he is a liar and the father of lies"* (John 8:44, NLT). The Devil is the father of lies and he will do anything to deceive us and get us off our destined path. Therefore, Jesus cautions us, *"Be careful that no one misleads you [deceiving you and leading you into error]"* (Matthew 24:4, AMP).

We can easily be misled if we are not grounded in the Word of God, the Holy Bible. The Apostle Paul warns, *"Don't let anyone lead you astray with empty philosophy and high-sounding nonsense that comes from human thinking and from the evil power of this world"* (Colossians 2:8, NLT). The evil power of this world is the Devil. The Devil would have us remain ignorant of God's Word so we never come to know the truth and therefore never really come to know the One True God.

We have seen in the past where church congregations who were discouraged from reading their Bibles were easily led astray. Therefore, Christians must be alert as the Apostle Paul warns, *"Even from your own number men will arise and distort the truth in order to draw away disciples after them. So be on your guard"* (Acts 20:30-31a, NIV)! Again, it is the Word of God and the Spirit that will guide us into all truth. When we put our faith in God and trust Him, we will have peace.

PEACE

Jesus tells us that though there is trouble in the world, in Him we may have peace. Jesus said, *"But take heart! I have overcome the world"* (John 16:33b, NIV). The Devil, who operates in the world, tries to disrupt us from living in peace, but Jesus is telling us that in Him we may live in peace. God gave me a simple illustration of how the Devil tries to disrupt our peace in this next dream. In my dream I saw huge flies buzzing all around my head and face and flying into my hair.

Disgusted, I was swinging and swatting at these flies; then I awoke. Interestingly, in 2 Kings 1:2, the Devil is referred to as Baalzebub[5] which translates as *"lord of the fly."* Through this dream, I realized I was allowing the frustrations and irritations of life to get to me, and I needed to keep my focus and attention on God to keep my peace.

As we read earlier, we are to pray about everything, but the Apostle Paul then continues to tell us how we may keep our peace. *"Don't worry about anything; instead, pray about everything. Tell God what you need, and thank Him for all He has done. Then you will experience God's peace, which exceeds anything we can understand. His peace will guard your hearts and minds as you live in Christ Jesus"* (Philippians 4:6-7, NLT).

Many years ago, I was really frustrated about a mistaken corrective surgery that I'd had which made my condition worse. After seeking the counsel of several other surgeons, I was told nothing could be done to correct the mistake. This situation was stealing my peace, so I prayed, and God gave me a dream telling me to do "twenty days of prayer." On my first night of prayer, the Lord showed me that I had two different streams of thoughts. On one side, I was feeling hopeless and angry. On the other side, I was giving the offense to the Lord—casting this care of mine to Him. When I woke up, I realized that God was presenting me with a choice.

As I continued with my twenty days of prayer, I began to lift my condition up to God. This helped me to focus on God and not my problem. *"You will keep in perfect peace him whose mind is steadfast, because he trusts in You"* (Isaiah 26:3, NIV). By the end of the twenty days, I found I had a more peaceful perspective. Jesus tells us, *"Peace I leave with you; My (perfect) peace I give to you; not as the world gives do I give to you. Do not let* *your heart be troubled, nor let it be afraid. [**Let My perfect peace calm you in every circumstance and give you courage and strength for every challenge**]"* (John 14:27, AMP). No matter what our situation, when we put our trust in Him, the result will be peace of mind.

THE HELMET OF SALVATION

When Jesus was with the disciples, He began to explain that He *"must go to Jerusalem and suffer many things at the hands of the elders, chief priests, and teachers of the law, and that He must be killed and on the third day be raised to life. Peter took Him aside and began to rebuke Him. 'Never, Lord,' he said. 'This shall never happen to you!' Jesus turned and said to Peter, '**Get behind Me Satan!** You are a stumbling block to Me; you do not have in mind the things of God, but the things of men'"* (Matthew 16:21-23, NIV). It would appear that Peter was being protective of Jesus (and perhaps of himself), but he did not understand that it was God's will for Jesus to die on the cross for the forgiveness of all sin. Jesus, however, had His mind firmly established on the things of God. He did not want to let the thought of escaping the cross even enter His mind. Likewise, we are to wear our helmet of salvation with such determination.

Recently, I was unable to sleep because I was concerned about many things and many people. I asked the Lord about this, and I had a dream. In my dream, I looked behind me, and I saw the Devil standing with a spear through his heart. At the moment I saw him, I began to free fall; I fell and fell and fell uncontrollably, and then I awoke. I believe the Lord was showing me that the Devil was behind me, **and he was pierced by the Word of God, *but*** I was not sleeping because of fear and anxiety. I realized I needed to protect my thoughts to prevent my mind from free falling into worry.

81

The Apostle Paul writes, *"We demolish arguments and every pretension that sets itself up against the knowledge of God, and we take captive every THOUGHT to make it obedient to Christ"* (2 Corinthians 10:5, NIV).

Interestingly, my son had a dream where he saw spiders trying to crawl into his mouth, and he was swiping them away. Then he looked over at someone who was purposely eating these spiders. As he was telling me this dream, the Lord showed me the spiders were symbolic of what we are choosing to THINK about. Evidently, if you eat a poisonous spider, you may not die, but it can make you very sick. This person in his dream who was purposefully eating these spiders was choosing to THINK on wrong things, and as a result, began to struggle with bouts of depression and serious health issues. Philippians 4:8 (NIV), tells us to think on *"whatever is true, whatever is noble, whatever is right, whatever is pure, whatever is lovely, whatever is admirable—if anything is excellent or praiseworthy—think about such things."* We are to think on these things because they are God's character and nature.

As we take hold of what God says in His Word, we begin to understand His enormous love for us, His will, and His ways for our lives. Our mind, will, and emotions will be renewed, and we will begin to change from our old thinking to the mind of Christ.

> *"For who has known the mind and purposes of the Lord,*
> *so as to instruct Him?* **But we have the mind of Christ**
> *[to be guided by His thoughts and purposes]."*
> 1 Corinthians 2:16, AMP

In this transformation, our new self (our new creation) in Christ is strengthened and equipped as we grow in our faith. Verse 9 of Philippians 4 continues to say that if we put into practice what we have learned, God's peace will be with us. Therefore, we must set our minds on God as this next dream illustrates. In this dream I was flying in a small plane. The plane had three rows of seats, and I was in the very back row of the plane. Suddenly, the plane became very unsteady. I had to struggle to get over each row of seats and finally make my way to the front of the plane. Then I awoke. In this dream, I felt the front of the plane was my mind. I needed to get control of my thoughts and stay on the course God had planned for me. To do this, I had several distracting hurdles to overcome. Sometimes we have to fight off distractions so we can focus on what is truly important to God.

When the enemy tries to attack our mind, we must stand firm in who we are as a child of Almighty God. The Apostle Paul encourages us to embrace the love the Father God and Jesus have for each of us and writes:

> *"Who shall separate us from the love of Christ? Shall trouble or hardship or persecution or famine or nakedness or danger or sword? As it is written: 'For your sake we face death all day long, we are considered as sheep to be slaughtered.' No, in all these things* **we are more than conquerors through Him who loved us.** *For I am convinced that neither death nor life, neither angels nor demons, neither the present nor the future, nor any powers, neither height nor depth, nor anything else in all creation, will be able to separate us from the love of God that is in Christ Jesus our Lord."*
> Romans 8:35-39, NIV

It is in Jesus Christ, with the revelation of the Holy Spirit, that we may come to know we are precious, deeply loved, and valued by God. Knowing this helps protect our mind from the attacks and tauntings of the enemy: the Devil and his demons.

THE BREASTPLATE OF RIGHTEOUSNESS

The final piece of the armor of God is the breastplate of righteousness. Through belief in and receiving of Jesus Christ, we are forgiven of our sins and made in right standing with the Father, God. As we embrace His great love for us and continue in the Word of God, we begin to be changed, renewed, and transformed as we become more and more like Jesus Christ. Just as a soldier's breastplate covers the soldier's heart when going into battle, we are to protect and safeguard the precious treasure of Jesus Christ with our breastplate of righteousness. We can protect ourselves and stay close to God by living in His righteousness through choosing to live a prayerful and fasted lifestyle.

PRAYER: LIVING A PRAYERFUL LIFESTYLE

As stated earlier, we are to wear the full armor of God as described above and *"pray in the Spirit on all occasions with all kinds of prayers and requests."* The importance of prayer is discussed in Chapter 3, but now let us look at the importance of prayer as it relates to protecting us from evil, specifically from the Devil and his demons.

Jesus mentions the power of prayer as a means of protection on several occasions and warns us to watch and pray. *"Pray that you will not fall into temptation"* (Luke 22:40, NIV). And Jesus tells us to pray, *"Lead us not into temptation, but deliver us from the evil one"* (Matthew 6:13, NIV). In Acts 16:25-26 (NIV), Paul and Silas witnessed the power of prayer to deliver them from bondage. In this passage, Paul and Silas were imprisoned for preaching the message of Jesus Christ. The Bible recounts their prison experience:

"About midnight Paul and Silas were praying and singing hymns to God, and the other prisoners were listening to them. Suddenly there was such a violent earthquake that the foundations of the prison were shaken. At once all the prison doors flew open, and everybody's chains came loose."

Paul and Silas were faithful even while in prison to praise, worship, and pray to God. This was because they had made prayer an ever-present lifestyle! God heard their prayers, loosed them from their bondage, and set them free.

Through praise, worship, and prayer, we can embrace a godly perspective of who He is, which shifts our focus from our situation to the greatness of God that overcomes the works of the Devil through Jesus Christ. Many years ago, my husband began to have a sore throat, and the Lord impressed him to take authority over the sore throat. God gave him a vision of a glass container full of liquid with stones resting at the bottom. These stones represented the sickness. To get the stones out of the container, he had to stir up the liquid and force the stones up and out. Jim saw God's will in the spirit realm and knew what he needed to do. He stirred up his faith through praise, worship, and prayer, and the sickness lifted. When we are delivered or rescued from the works of the Devil, that is deliverance. In this case, the works of the Devil was the sickness (infirmity).

Psalm 145:1-7 (NIV) so beautifully gives us an example of how we may stir up our faith:

"I will extol You, my God the King; I will praise Your name forever and ever. Every day I will praise You and extol Your name forever and ever. Great is the Lord and most worthy of praise; His greatness no one can fathom. One generation will command Your works to another;

they will tell of Your mighty acts. They will speak of the glorious splendor of Your majesty, and I will meditate on Your wonderful works. They will tell of the power of Your awesome works, and I will proclaim Your great deeds. They will celebrate Your abundant goodness and joyfully sing of Your righteousness."

The Apostle Paul tells us to make prayer a way of life—a lifestyle—and wrote to the Thessalonians, *"Rejoice always,* **pray without ceasing,** *in everything give thanks; for this is the will of God in Christ Jesus for you"* (1 Thessalonians 5:16-18, NKJV).

FASTING—LIVING A FASTED LIFESTYLE

As mentioned in Chapter 3, fasting can be to abstain from something for spiritual purposes, such as to abstain from food and/or drink. Living a fasted lifestyle, in part, is to fast from our own will and to instead obey the Father God's will. The heart of fasting is intended to turn our attention to God, making Him our focus first and foremost in our life.[6] Put simply, fasting gives us the opportunity to acknowledge God when we would normally be doing as we please! When we put God first through fasting/living a fasted lifestyle, we can, among many things, develop willpower, discipline, and self-control. This is important because learning restraint will help us to resist the temptations of the Devil when they come our way. Jesus said to Peter, *"Keep watch and pray, so that you will not give in to temptation. For the spirit is willing, but the body is weak"* (Matthew 26:41, NLT)! Prayer and fasting—living a righteous lifestyle—strengthens us to stand against the temptations of this world.

The Bible gives many examples of those who lived a righteous lifestyle and therefore had the self-discipline to resist temptation, as well as those who did not. I am reminded of Samson in the Old Testament. God had blessed him with a great gift of physical strength. In reading about Samson in Judges 14-16, it seems to me that even though the Spirit of the LORD came upon him in power, Samson lived an indulgent lifestyle. He fell prey to the lusts of the flesh, and he did as he pleased (Judges 16:1). Further, he and the Philistines, the enemy of Samson's people, were always avenging each other; therefore, the Philistines relentlessly pursued him. So, the Philistines, knowing Samson's weakness for women, paid a beautiful woman named Delilah to tempt him into revealing the source of his strength so that they could capture him (Judges 16:19). Three times Samson was able to mislead her and avoid being captured, but on the fourth attempt, he told Delilah the secret to his strength was in cutting his hair. Then when Samson fell asleep, his hair was cut, and the Philistines were able to take him captive.

Though Samson was very gifted by God, God allowed the consequences of his actions to come upon him, and the Lord left him (Judges 16:20). But God was merciful and later restored Samson's strength and used him to destroy the Philistine rulers by collapsing the two central pillars of the temple where they stood. Many Philistines were killed, and Samson died as well. Though he ultimately fulfilled his purpose, he suffered a horrible end.

Now compare the life of Samson to the life of Daniel of the Old Testament. Daniel was raised under Jewish law, where he submitted to a prayerful and fasted lifestyle. As a young adult, Daniel was taken captive by King Nebuchadnezzar of Babylon. Many of the captives, including Daniel, were being trained to serve in the king's court. Even under captivity, Daniel faithfully prayed to God. Further, he and his three friends asked for a diet that consisted of fruits, vegetables, and water (today known as the Daniel Fast). Hebraic law allowed for certain meats, but Daniel did not want to *"defile himself with the royal food and wine"* (Daniel 1:8, NIV). They were given favor and permitted to do so, and they were prosperous. *"To these four young men God gave knowledge and understanding of all kinds of literature and learning. And Daniel could understand visions and dreams of all kinds"* (Daniel 1:17, NIV). The four were allowed to continue their lifestyle of prayer and fasting. The king, who did not know Daniel's God, said to Daniel, *"I have heard that the spirit of the gods is in you and that you have insight, intelligence, and outstanding wisdom"* (Daniel 5:14, NIV). Shortly thereafter, Daniel was put in a position of great authority. In this position, he could have easily taken advantage of the people and/or misused funds, but he did not. *"Now Daniel so distinguished himself among the administrators and the satraps by his exceptional qualities that the king planned to set him over the whole kingdom. At this, the administrators and the satraps tried to find grounds for charges against Daniel in his conduct of government affairs, but they were unable to do so. They could find no corruption in him because he was trustworthy and neither corrupt nor negligent"* (Daniel 6:3-4, NIV).

Notice the difference between Samson and Daniel. I believe the difference is that Daniel was trained to live a prayerful and fasted lifestyle from his youth. He had learned to say NO to the indulgences of life's temptations at an early age. Daniel chose to live a righteous lifestyle which allowed him to live a peaceful life.

CHOOSE TO LIVE A FASTED LIFESTYLE

When our son was very young, he had a dream where the Lord revealed to him that some of his action toys were a "flair of the Devil." I thought this wording was very unusual for a five-year-old, so I paid close attention. Even though he had enjoyed playing with these toys, he quickly threw them away. And we need to do the same—get rid of anything that is not pleasing to God. We see in Matthew 21:12-13 that Jesus cleaned out His environment when He cleaned out the temple.

Then, on another occasion, our son dreamed he wanted to play a particular video game. As always, he looked on the box to see what it was rated. He saw the rating "Opening Doors." Then he awoke from his dream. As he was telling me this dream, I knew exactly what it meant. The Lord was telling him that some video games contain content that would be like opening the door to the Devil and his demons to torment his mind. The Apostle Paul tells us that although things may be permissible, *"Not everything is good for you . . . and not everything is beneficial"* (1 Corinthians 10:23, NLT). Therefore, we must be alert and obey warnings from the Lord. This sometimes means doing what we know will be pleasing to the Lord over what we want to do.

As the years passed, similar situations would happen where the Lord would have our son throw away certain movies, books, video games, and the like. Though this began from a young age, we always allowed him to be the one to throw these items away. What I didn't realize at the time was that God was training him (and us as parents) to hear the Lord's voice so we could obey Him. He was teaching us to be prayerful and fasted—how to live a righteous lifestyle.

Perhaps some of us did not have the benefit of being trained up in the way we should live our life, or perhaps we have gotten off-track along the way. We can change all that by turning to God, and with His guidance, we can begin to live a prayerful and fasted lifestyle. The following story is from a friend who took steps to change his life and break away from his old lifestyle to live a righteous lifestyle. He was greatly strengthened and now lives a peaceful, happy life. He writes in his own words:

> "I was raised in a strong, Christian home but somehow my life got off-track, and I took on many addictions, one of them being pornography. Though I knew God's truths, I had chosen to disregard them.
>
> *The LORD detests the way of the wicked but he loves those who pursue righteousness. Stern discipline awaits him who leaves the path; he who hates correction will die.'*
> Proverbs 15:9-10, NIV
>
> Then one evening, a woman confronted me and said, 'The Lord says your life is evil.' Somehow, those words pierced my heart, and I gave my life to Jesus Christ. That night, I walked away from my entire life. Unfortunately, I found myself with no friends, no relationships, and no idea how to live the choice I'd just made. I realized that I was completely dependent on God for protection.
>
> I know God wanted me to change my life, so over the next eighteen months, He rebuilt me piece-by-piece. I praise God for His living Word—the Bible—for a wonderful church that welcomed me in and was God's love to

me on Earth. And for a men's Bible study that did not judge my brokenness, for a family who loved and prayed for me throughout, and for the guidance and comfort of the Holy Spirit. (Read Psalm 34:17-19.)

It is important to realize that deliverance is not in your own strength. You are delivered and able to live free through Jesus Christ and God by the Spirit working in you. You must believe deliverance is real. With God, you are empowered to live and walk in complete freedom. Freedom came over time as the Lord renewed my heart and mind.

I came to realize that what God was really seeking from me was to be in relationship with Him. In this, true life and true love can be found. You can begin by simply asking God to reveal His love for you today. Not only did He grant me the gift of salvation, but my life is nothing if not a testimony to His love, His faithfulness, and His restoration."

My friend prayerfully continued in his faith by seeking Jesus and meditating on the Word of God, and with the help of the Spirit, he came to know the love of the Father God. God's love created in him a desire and ability to break free from his addictions. Proverbs 21:21 (NLT) promises, *"Whoever pursues righteousness and unfailing love will find life, righteousness, and honor."*

In Luke 8:1-2 (NIV), we see Mary Magdalene was delivered from seven spirits by Jesus. What a blessing; she encountered Jesus and was set free. If we are bound by any stronghold or feel pressed daily where our soul is vexed unto death (as Samson felt about Delilah in Judges 16:16, KJV), the good news is that Jesus Christ came to preach deliverance to set the captives free.

I have a friend who was in a highly-addictive situation. The Lord showed me how she could be set free. In my dream, my friend had weeds, which were entangled and deeply rooted, growing out of her veins from the inside of her arm. In Matthew 13:38-41, weeds represent evil and those who do evil. Sadly, my friend's addiction was to an unhealthy relationship with a man (you could say she was vexed by him). He treated my friend horribly and obviously did not know how to love her, yet she could not give him up. In the dream, we were trying to pull the weeds out, but my friend was in tremendous pain, so we stopped. But when we prayed and asked God to help in the name of Jesus Christ, the weeds began to be loosened and come out with ease (Mark 9:29, NIV). The Lord set her free—Amen!

When my friend accepted the love found in our Heavenly Father God, she was able to break free by the name and power of Jesus Christ. When we cannot do it on our own, God will strengthen us and provide a way of escape (Hebrews 2:18). Apostle Paul wrote, *"No temptation has overtaken you except such as is common to man; but God is faithful, who will not allow you to be tempted beyond what you are able, but with the temptation will also make the way of escape, that you may be able to bear it"* (1 Corinthians 10:13, NKJV).

Have you noticed that the enemy will try to tempt us in an area where we seem the weakest? This is what the above scripture refers to as when it says *"common to man."* The Lord showed me an example of this in the life of a friend who struggled with alcoholism. I had a dream that a thief was coming into her home to destroy and steal at will. I saw wide open gaps in her fence that surrounded her home so the enemy had easy access.

Shortly thereafter, I had another dream. In my dream, we were taken back to the home she had grown up in as a child. As we went into this house, I saw a demon lurking in a doorway. I asked the demon, "What are you doing here? How did you get in?" The demon then began to recoil, and I awoke. With these two dreams, I knew a demon had harassed my friend from a young age (and perhaps her family for generations before her). As cited in chapter 1, God said to Cain, *"Sin is crouching at your door; it desires to have you, but you must master it"* (Genesis 4:6-7, NIV). My friend needed to close off all open doors and entryways to the Devil and his demons to protect herself and her family.

Because my friend was now born into the family of Almighty God, she could live out her life as a new creation. With Jesus Christ, we are set free. Then by continuing in the Word, and with the revelation of the Holy Spirit, we can choose to live a prayerful and fasted lifestyle. In this, we are creating a strong breastplate of righteousness of the armor of God which will cover and protect our heart.

"Above all else, guard your heart,
for ***everything you do*** *flows from it."*
Proverbs 4:23, NIV

God is so good; He gives us all this armor to protect and defend ourselves against the schemes of the Devil and his demons. Yet so many believers continue to suffer from addictions and depression and live defeated lives. In a dream, I was told three reasons people are unable to overcome the Devil and his demons.

1. People willingly sin.

Though people know they are sinning, they choose to continue to sin. Rather than choosing to embrace God's love and live in His righteousness, many choose to engage in (what the Bible calls) evil. Sadly, these people have surrendered to sin rather than yielding to God and His plan for their life (Romans 6). The Apostle Paul explains in Romans 1:18-20 (NLT), *"God shows His anger from heaven against all sinful, wicked people who suppress the truth by their wickedness. They know the truth about God because He has made it obvious to them. For ever since the world was created, people have seen the earth and sky. Through everything God made, they can clearly see His invisible qualities—His eternal power and divine nature. So, they have no excuse for not knowing God."*

2. People have apathy for God.

Unfortunately, people do not know that in God—The Father, The Son (The Word), and The Spirit—we have power and authority over the works of the Devil and his demons. Jesus came to destroy the works of the Devil by His death on the cross (1 John 3:8). He was resurrected from the dead, and this same resurrection power that raised Jesus Christ from the dead lives in us. Through Jesus Christ, continuing to walk with Him, and staying in the written-living Word of God, along with the help of the Holy Spirit, we are equipped to overcome and live a victorious life. Because people do not have this understanding and knowledge of the power available to them, they have apathy for God. But with the righteousness of God in Jesus Christ operating in us, we may overcome the works of the Devil and overpower the influence of sin in our lives.

LIKE LEMONS, DEMONS TRY TO SOUR EVERYTHING

3. People do not put God first in their life.

When God is not first in our life, it means we have made someone or something other than God the center of our life. This could be money, social media, technology, sports, or our career, for example. But God loves us so much that He wants us to be with Him and be passionately in love with Him. The first of the Ten Commandments is, *"You shall have no other gods before Me"* (Exodus 20:3, NIV). A few years after my husband and I were married, we went to Egypt and brought back several painted Egyptian images and hung them on the walls of our home. Shortly thereafter, I had a dream to remove them. We had paid a lot of money for them, and after some discussion, these items remained in our home! Then I had another dream. In this dream, I saw a large gavel motioning downward, and I heard these words, "And a curse shall come upon . . . " I awoke at that moment. God made His point clear! He did not want even a remnant of these worldly gods in our home. We removed and destroyed those Egyptian items that very day. Though we had no attachment to these items, God wanted them out of our home, so we needed to obey. In our obedience, we were showing God that He was first above anything in our lives. God loves us, and He wants us to love Him first and foremost.

Through this dream, I was told that the greatest reason people do not overcome the Devil and his demons is apathy. People are apathetic because they do not know the authority, power, and strength they can draw on from Jesus Christ to overcome the Devil and his demons.

John, who wrote Revelation, was exiled to an island called Patmos for his belief in Jesus Christ. He wrote of how we may overcome the Devil in Revelation 12:10b-11 (NKJV), *" ... for the accuser of our brethren, who accused them before our God day and night, has been cast down. And they overcame him by the blood of the Lamb and by the word of their testimony, and they did not love their lives to the death."* Likewise, we also may overcome the enemy (the Devil and his demons) with:

~ The blood of the Lamb, Jesus Christ,
~ The Word of our testimony, and
~ To love not our own lives [even] unto death.

THE BLOOD OF THE LAMB

Jesus Christ is the Lamb of God. John, the cousin of Jesus, said upon seeing Jesus, *"Look, the Lamb of God, who takes away the sin of the world"* (John 1:29, NIV)! Jesus is the sacrificial Lamb who shed His blood on the cross to take our sins away (1 John 4:9 NLT). Our belief in Jesus Christ and receiving Him as our Lord and Savior is the foundational truth essential to overcoming the Devil and his demons (1 John 5:10-12). Jesus, being the Son of God, is God's rightful heir. God sent His Son to save us but also to defeat the works of the Devil as the Apostle Paul explains in Colossians 2:13-15 (NLT).

> *"You were dead because of your sins and because your sinful nature was not yet cut away. Then God made you alive with Christ, for He forgave all our sins. He canceled the record of the charges against us and took it away by nailing it to the cross. In this way,* **He disarmed the spiritual rulers and authorities. He shamed them publicly by His victory over them on the cross."**

96

The Devil does not want us to know this truth. He tries to make us think he and his demons are more powerful than God, but the above Scripture tells us God disarmed the spiritual rulers and authorities by the shed blood of Jesus Christ on the cross—the blood of the Lamb.

THE WORD OF OUR TESTIMONY

A biblical definition of testimony is a "declaration of truth, based on personal experience."[7] We read in the Bible that the Sanhedrin Jews told the Apostles Peter and John to never speak of Jesus again because they did not want the message of Jesus Christ to spread throughout the land. Their response was: *"We cannot stop telling about everything we have seen and heard"* (Acts 4:20, NLT). Their personal experience compelled them to tell others about Jesus.

Likewise, the power, impact, influence, and effect of Jesus in us creates and becomes our personal testimony. There is a testimony in the Bible of a *"demon-plagued man"* who was so tormented by evil spirits that he did not wear clothes and lived in isolation for a long time. Jesus set this man free from the demons harassing him, and the people of the area *"found the man from whom the demons had gone—clothed and in his right mind"* (Luke 8:35, TLV). A demon had a tormenting grip on this man's mind, but Jesus delivered him and set him free.

Recall that Jesus explained in John 8:36 (NIV), *"If the Son sets you free, you will be free indeed."* Jesus set this *"demon-plagued man"* free. Then when it was time for Jesus to move on, *"The man from whom the demons had gone out begged to go with Him, but Jesus sent him away, saying, 'Return home and **tell how much God has done for you.'** So the man went away and told all over town how much Jesus had done for him"* (Luke 8:38-39, NIV).

Remember, it is in and through Jesus Christ that we are delivered from darkness and brought into a new life. Our new life then becomes a living testimony of Him. This is the word of our testimony. Our personal testimony is very valuable because victory in Jesus Christ goes beyond ourselves. When we become a living testimony of how Jesus changed our life, it will cause others to want to know Jesus so they, too, may be saved from the tormenting grip of the Devil and his demons.

In my early twenties, I was in a car accident in which my leg, ankle, and heel were severely injured and required seven reconstructive surgeries. Consequently, over time, arthritis had begun to develop in my ankle joint, and I was in constant pain. Then one day in a church service, the pastor said for everyone with arthritis to come forward or stand. Many did so, including me, and then he commanded the arthritis pain to leave in the name of Jesus Christ. Just as quickly as a snap my pain was gone! It is hard to describe, but my ankle just felt numb. Instantly, I had no pain at all, and I have been pain-free for over twenty years. My Aunt Ellen, who was sitting with me, was also healed of arthritis pain in her neck. This is now our personal testimony of how we were delivered from arthritis pain through the authority and power of the name of Jesus Christ.

Notice that this pastor was not commanding God to take the arthritis pain away. We cannot command God to do anything! Rather, he was commanding the spirit of infirmity/disabling spirit to leave by the authority and power in the name of Jesus Christ. Jesus delivered a woman from a spirit of infirmity/disabling spirit in Luke 13:11-13.

Jesus had such godly authority and power by His word that unclean spirits would obey His command. People were amazed by this. *"What a word is this! For with authority and power He [speaking of Jesus] commands the unclean spirits, and they come out"* (Luke 4:36, NKJV). The Devil and his demons try to harass, afflict, and sour everything in our lives, but because of Jesus' death and resurrection, we have victory in and through Him.

> *"Yet it was because of this that God raised Him up to the heights of heaven and gave Him a name which is above every other name, that at the name of Jesus every knee shall bow in heaven and on earth and under the earth, and every tongue shall confess that Jesus Christ is Lord, to the glory of God the Father."*
> Philippians 2:9-11, TLB

In Mark 4:39 (NKJV), Jesus spoke to the wind during a storm, *"'Peace, be still,' and the waves ceased and there was great calm."* We are to do the same—by the authority and power in the name of Jesus Christ. Many years ago, a friend began to have random bouts of pain and pressure in her chest. Using wisdom, she went to the doctor and was told it was an anxiety attack. Then, one night, as she began to have pain in her chest, her faith rose up, and she commanded the attack to stop in the name of Jesus Christ. The power of Jesus Christ rose up in her, and the attack stopped! The Apostle Paul explains what happened: *"Submit yourselves, then, to God. Resist the devil, and he will flee from you. Come near to God and He will come near to you"* (James 4:7-8a, NIV).

Perhaps you feel you don't have this kind of faith to be set free, but God wants us to understand that the purest measure of faith, no matter how tiny, is extremely powerful. Jesus said, *"If you have faith as small as a mustard seed, **you can say** to this mulberry tree, 'Be uprooted and planted in the sea, and it will obey you'"* (Luke 17:6, NIV). Similarly, in Mark 11:23 (NIV), Jesus told his disciples, *"If anyone **says** to this mountain,*

'Go, throw yourself into the sea' and does not doubt in his heart but believes that what he says will happen, it will be done for him."

I saw an example of this firsthand when someone close to me was struggling with tremendous, overwhelming fear (1 John 4:18a). I prayed and prayed for him, but he was not set free. One night, it was so bad he called out to God for help and the Lord responded, "You are saved. I will stop the tormentors." In an instant, peace came over him. God Himself contended with His contender (Isaiah 49:25) and fear left. Psalm 34:4 (TLB) reads, *"For I cried to Him and He answered me! He freed me from all my fears."* And Isaiah 41:10 (NKJV) reads, *"Fear not, for I am with you; Be not dismayed, for I am your God. I will strengthen you, Yes, I will help you, I will uphold you with My righteous right hand."*

In a dream, I was in a very high building with glass windows on all sides. I watched as people would rush to the window to look down, and when they did this, fear overwhelmed them, and they fell out of the window to the ground. When I awoke, I was given the impression that if we stayed centered and focused on God, we would be safe and protected in Him. With our focus on God, we will not fall into fear.

In 2 Kings 6, the servant of Elisha became afraid when he woke up and saw an army with horses and chariots surrounding the city. *"And Elisha prayed, and said, 'LORD, I pray, open his eyes that he may see.' Then the LORD opened the eyes of the young man, and he saw. And behold, the mountain was full of horses and chariots of fire all around Elisha"* (2 Kings 6:17, NKJV). God was protecting them in a supernatural way. Still, the servant could not see this because he was looking only at the natural, which was bringing him great fear. But we can do

100

as Elisha did, look to God, and ask Him to open our eyes so we may see His will and His way in our situation.

When King David was betrayed by a close friend who intended to kill him, he wrote, *"Cast your cares on the LORD and He will sustain you; He will never let the righteous be shaken"* (Psalm 55:22, NIV). We can learn from King David to cast all our anxiety on God because He cares for us (1 Peter 5:7). God is a loving Father, and He wants us free of fear and all other tormenting spirits.

Our being set free and living free then becomes our testimony of God's greatness. The final step in overcoming the Devil and his demons, according to Revelation 12:10-11, is to live for God rather than for ourselves. I like the way the NIV translation reads: *"... they did not love their lives so much as to shrink from death."*

TO LOVE NOT OUR OWN LIFE [EVEN] UNTO DEATH

Christians are being martyred around the world for their faith. But most of us will not be asked to lay down our lives for Jesus' sake. For many of us, God is looking for a different kind of death, a death of our own selfish ways. This is to love God so much it causes us to lay down anything in our life that is contrary to Him, His will, and His ways. This is, in part, what Revelation 12:11 (NKJV) means when stating, *"They did not love their lives to the death."*

As we grow in our relationship with Jesus Christ, and He increases in us, we begin to break free from things that are not pleasing to God. This is what a dear friend did to overcome her struggle with a 25-year bulimic eating disorder. Her deliverance was gradual, but as Jesus began to increase in her, she became more and more able to resist the desire to

101

the point that she was fully free from her eating disorder. My friend said in her own words:

> "It took a lot of prayer, discipline, and steadfastness! A lot of falling down and getting back up and never giving up! You have to make a decision to live for Him, Jesus Christ, and die to yourself each day. The Holy Spirit has to help. Because you have to eat to live, you must be regimented and control that area of your life, one step at a time, until you finally break free of the stronghold."

A stronghold, in this regard, is a mindset that controls our behavior and is difficult to break free from on our own. My friend knew she needed more than human strategy to get free, so she turned to God and His abundant grace and was greatly strengthened (James 4:6). She would read over and over Scriptures such as:

~ *"Though he may stumble, he will not fall, for the Lord upholds him with His hand"* (Psalm 37:24, NIV).
~ *"Do not rejoice over me, my enemy; When I fall, I will arise; When I sit in darkness, The LORD will be a light to me"* (Micah 7:8, NKJV).

As my friend was increasing in Jesus through the Word of God, her addiction was decreasing (John 3:30). What she was doing was dying to herself (Matthew 16:24) and allowing God to come in and do a work in her life.

Though God can instantly deliver us, many of us will take back control over our lives little by little (Deuteronomy 7:22). I had a dream of another friend who was struggling with an addiction to alcohol for many years. In my dream, she appeared to me as a baby. She was like a baby because she felt utterly helpless and hopeless. My friend was reaching for an alcoholic drink but was given milk instead. I asked about this and was told it was unpasteurized, raw milk, and then I woke up. 1 Peter 2:2-3 (NKJV) tells us, *"... as newborn babes, desire the pure milk of the word, that you may grow thereby, if indeed you have tasted that the Lord is gracious."* The dream meant my friend needed to be fed the raw truths of the Word of God, and then little by little, she could grow and progress to solid foods and then to meat until she was made strong, stable, and healthy (1 Corinthians 3:2).

As we draw closer and closer to God, through the Word of God and with the help of the Holy Spirit, we will be strengthened. *"He makes my feet like the feet of deer, And sets me on my high places. He teaches my hands to make war, so that my arms can bend a bow of bronze"* (Psalm 18:33-34, NKJV). Similarly, 2 Samuel 22:35 (NKJV) reads, *"He teaches my hands to make war, So that my arms can bend a bow of bronze."*

This is what happened to my friends. As they began to walk out their new life in Jesus through the Word of God and with the power of the Holy Spirit, they were strengthened to follow God's will and ways. They did not love their own lives more than to follow God's ways and humbly chose to live for Him.

BE HUMBLE AS JESUS WAS HUMBLE

The Apostle Paul wrote about Jesus' total act of humility. *"Your attitude should be the kind that was shown us by Jesus Christ, ... He humbled Himself ... as actually to die a criminal's death on a cross"* (Philippians 2:5-8, TLB). As mentioned earlier, when we are in complete obedience to the leading of the Lord (the

Spirit), this is true humility. Jesus humbly obeyed the will of the Father—even to the point of death on a cross.

How was Jesus able to maintain the right attitude and have the ability to humbly obey? As discussed in Chapter 3, Jesus had the Spirit and Glory to affirm Him in going to the cross. Jesus also knew He was dearly loved by His Father (Matthew 3:16-17)[8], and He knew with certainty the will of His Father (Luke 9:30-31).[9]

Likewise, in confidently knowing the love of the Father God and His perfect will for our lives, we can respond willingly and in loving obedience. The Apostle Paul wrote, *"I have been crucified with Christ and I no longer live, but Christ lives in me. The life I now live in the body, I live by faith in the Son of God, who loved me and gave Himself for me"* (Galatians 2:20, NIV). Notice that Paul said he knew he was loved, and he knew that Jesus' humble act and enormous sacrifice of going to the cross was for him personally. Paul received Jesus with such depth, he no longer wanted to live for himself, but instead he wanted to live for Christ alone. This exchange, our living for God versus living for ourselves, is the ultimate in loving not our own lives even unto death. When we comprehend and receive His great love for us, this changes everything, and we will willingly and eagerly want to follow the will and ways of God.

In John 5:6 (NIV), Jesus asks a crippled man, *"Do you want to get well?"* Jesus' question is interesting. Just as God gives us a choice to believe and receive Jesus unto salvation, God gives us a free choice to live in His righteousness. We do not know the details of this crippled man's condition, but we do know he was bound by something, and Jesus set him free and told him, *"Get up. Pick up your mat and walk"* (John 5:8, NIV). The Bible tells us Jesus later found this man in the temple. *"See, you are well again. Stop sinning or something worse may come upon you"* (John 5:14, NIV). Obviously, something was in this man's life that he needed to lay down (perhaps some sort of addiction), and Jesus is encouraging him to stay free so nothing worse will come upon him.

I have another friend who was struggling with an adulterous relationship she knew was not pleasing to God. She had severed the relationship but was thinking about going back to this sinful lifestyle. One night, the Lord gave her a dream where she saw a house, and in the house was a monster with many long-necked heads. It's scary to even imagine! The Lord revealed to her that if she went back to this adulterous relationship, she would be opening the door for this monstrous demon to torment her mind. The Lord said to her, "Who are you going to serve?" (Read Joshua 24:15.) The Lord made His point! God was telling her she must choose who she was going to serve. This is why when we get free, we must be sure to be filled with God to stay free.

> *"When an impure spirit comes out of a person, it goes*
> *through arid places seeking rest and does not find*
> *it. Then it says, 'I will return to the house I left.'*
> *When it arrives, it finds the house unoccupied, swept*
> *clean and put in order. Then it goes and takes with it*
> *seven other spirits more wicked than itself, and they go*
> *in and live there. And the final condition of that*
> *person is worse than the first."*
> Matthew 12:43-45a, NIV

In this Scripture passage, the house represents a person, and the unclean spirit is a demon. This house/person was swept clean, and the demon left, meaning that the person was delivered. But because they did not get filled with God, the demon came back with other spirits making it worse than before. This sounds like the image the Lord gave my friend of a house with a monster having many long-necked heads living in her mind. If my friend returned to the adulterous relationship, her mind would be tormented worse than before. Thankfully, my friend chose to serve the Lord. Today, she is free from that relationship and happily married.

We must be aware of the Devil's constant attempt to draw us back into our old lifestyle. The Bible encourages us to stand firm and not take back the Devil's yoke that controls us. *"It is for freedom that Christ has set us free. Stand firm, then, and do not let yourselves be burdened again by a yoke of slavery"* (Galatians 5:1, NIV). This is slavery to any stronghold that controls us. Remember, God wants us to master sin, not let sin master us.

The Apostle John tells us how we can stay free and live free. *"You, dear children, are from God and have overcome them, because the one who is in you is greater than the one who is in the world"* (1 John 4:4, NIV). This is what is needed to overcome the Devil and his demons—Jesus needs to be greater in us than anything in this world!

HOW DO WE GET MORE OF JESUS IN US?

Many years ago, I had a relative (who has since passed away) who was addicted to smoking. He put his mind to stop smoking, but the temptation was very great. One day he really wanted to smoke, and he heard a voice say, "Feed me." He was stunned to hear this, but this addiction had a real hold on him. Every time he gave into smoking, he was feeding that addiction. At that moment, he realized he needed to get free, and he could do this by feeding on Jesus. Jesus stated, *"Just as the living Father sent Me and I live because of the Father, **so the one who feeds on Me will live because of Me"*** (John 6:57, NIV).

Feeding on Jesus is how we get more of Jesus in us. One way we can feed on Jesus is through the act of Communion. The word *communion* means communing.[10] This is communing with, as in union or fellowship. It is a remembrance of the sacrifice Jesus Christ made for my sins and for your sins—for the redemption of all mankind. In Luke 22, we read about Jesus' words at His last supper with the disciples just before He submitted Himself to the Roman soldiers to be crucified. Jesus took a cup of wine and told them to share it, and He took bread saying, *"This is My body given for you; do this in remembrance of Me"* (Luke 22:19, NIV). The NLT reads, *"Do this to remember Me."*

We are to do the same today. We are to remind ourselves that His shed blood and body sacrifice was for each of us personally, and we remember this through the act of Holy Communion.

At one time I was struggling with some health challenges. Then one night the Lord gave me an interesting dream. In the dream I was in church, and I was trying to make my way to the altar in an effort to get closer to God. Along the way, I started slipping and sliding from side to side, and someone from the altar told me I could "tear off a piece of Communion," and I did, then I awoke.

Because of this dream, I began to have Communion very often, and I would say, "May This body and blood be to the nourishment of my body." As time passed, I would forget to take Communion. Then, one day, I heard the Lord say, "Did you take your bread?" Jesus tells us in John 6:35 that He is the *"bread of life."* The bread of life—Jesus Christ—sustains us spiritually, mentally, and physically. These words reenergized me to see the benefits of Holy Communion.

For me personally, I envision Jesus on the cross for my sins, my sicknesses, and all my worries (Isaiah 53). I say, "Because of Your sacrifice, I receive forgiveness, healing, and peace." And I pray whatever is on my heart, but the point is to never forget the price Jesus paid for us on the cross and to take in more and more of Jesus so we can live an abundant life every single day.

The Father God is so wonderfully good to us; He extends the offer of His love and of His Son, along with the help of the Holy Spirit, so we may overcome the Devil and his demons. *"For all the fullness of Deity lives bodily in Him, and in Him you have been filled to fullness. He is head over every ruler and authority"* (Colossians 2:9-10, TLV). This includes being head over the Devil and his demons.

In addition to having Communion, we can also feed on the Word of God, which helps us come to know the Living Word, Jesus Christ. We have talked much about this, but reading the Word of God for ourselves is highly important. One night, I had a dream of a woman I had known many years ago. In my dream, she was extremely emaciated. This person had a severe addiction to gossip and judgment. While in my dream, I said to this woman, "Oh, are you okay?" She replied: "No, I am very ill." The Lord let me see that though she went to church every Sunday and considered herself to be very socially religious, she was spiritually dying (as shown by being emaciated). The Lord was letting me see that she was spiritually ill because she was not feeding for herself on the Living Word, Jesus Christ, through the Word of God—the Holy Bible.

Just as actual food nourishes our bodies, the Word of God nourishes our spirits. In 3 John 1:2 (NLT), the apostle tells us: *"Dear friend, I hope all is well with you and that you are as healthy in body as you are strong in spirit."* By feeding on Jesus through prayerfully continuing in the Word of God, we will be nourished and strengthened to overcome the works of the Devil and live in a way that is pleasing to God. When we let the Word penetrate our minds and hearts, it begins to have its full effect on our lives. The Apostle Paul wrote, *"I can do all things through Christ who strengthens me"* (Philippians 4:13, NKJV).

Without the Word of God and the help of the Holy Spirit, it will be difficult to defend ourselves against the attacks and lies of the Devil and his demons. One night our son had a dream that a bear was trying to kill him. I prayed about this, and then I had a dream. In this dream, I was told that as David in the Old Testament killed a bear at a young age and lived to tell of this victory, our son was also to remember his victories through Jesus Christ. The Devil would have our son ponder his struggles and lie to him about his future which was bringing fear. But the truth is that God loves him and has an amazing future for him and wants him to remember all that he has overcome and celebrate these victories. We see an example of this when David had been pursued by King Saul's men in 1 Samuel 21:8-9, NIV.

> *"David asked Ahimelek, 'Don't you have a spear or a sword here? I haven't brought my sword or any other weapon, because the king's mission was urgent.' The priest replied, 'The sword of Goliath the Philistine, whom you killed in the Valley of Elah, is here; it is wrapped in a cloth behind the ephod. If you want it, take it; there is no sword here but that one.' David said, 'There is none like it; give it to me.'"*

I love this! Just when he needed it, God equipped David with a weapon that reminded him of a past victory. David remembered this sword in his victory over Goliath, and this remembrance emboldened him for his next quest. Likewise, the Lord was telling me that as God encouraged David with his past victories, I was to encourage my son to focus on his victories, not his struggles.

We will be strengthened and encouraged as we each remember our personal victories in and through Jesus Christ. David had his sword as his weapon, and today our weapon is the sword of the Spirit which is the Word of God—The Holy Bible. By taking in more of Jesus through Communion and the Word of God, and as we follow the truth revealed to us by the Holy Spirit, we will be equipped and strengthened to be set free and live an abundant life in Him.

EQUIPPED TO OVERCOME AND FULFILL OUR MISSION

In John 4, the disciples asked Jesus if He wanted to eat. Jesus tells them, *"I have food to eat that you know nothing about. … My food is to do the will of the One who sent Me and to accomplish His work"* (John 4:32-34, TLV). John 6:27 (NLT) tells us, *"Don't be so concerned about perishable things like food. Spend your energy seeking the eternal life that the Son of Man can give you."* With Jesus in us, we can be strengthened to do the will of the Father God and accomplish His work on Earth.

Yet some people, rather than choosing to do the will of the Father God, choose to be an instrument of darkness and willfully choose to follow the Devil and his demons. Anyone who obeys the works of the devil to kill, steal, and destroy is choosing to be part of the kingdom of darkness. One night the Lord gave me a dream of a teenage boy who came right into our home wearing an all-black suit of armor. In one hand, he was holding a black breastplate, and in the other he was holding a semi-automatic gun. He set his gun down to put on his black breastplate. He said, "I'm going to kill you all." In desperation, I called out "Jesus!" and God moved on him. He stopped and his demeanor changed, and we began to calmly talk about Jesus. Then a teenage girl entered the room and said with no emotion, "Why haven't you done it yet?" (Meaning: Why haven't you killed them yet?) I looked back at the teen boy, and he was now wearing normal clothing. He looked down as if to think for a moment, and said, "Because, I'm not going to." Then they both left our home.

The Lord was allowing me to see the Devil's army in the spirit realm. The teenage boy and girl intruders in my dream looked like normal people. But when my spiritual eyes were opened, I saw that they had joined the powers of darkness and the forces of evil. *"For our struggle is not against flesh and blood, but against the rulers, against the authorities, against the powers of this dark world and against the spiritual forces of evil in the heavenly realms"* (Ephesians 6:12, NIV). I believe my dream is symbolic of how the enemy—the Devil—comes to kill, steal, and destroy, and he uses anyone who will come into agreement with him.

The Apostle Paul states it this way, *"Do not offer the parts of your body to sin, as instruments of wickedness, but rather offer yourselves to God, as those who have been brought from death to life; and offer the parts of your body to Him as instruments of righteousness"* (Romans 6:13, NIV). Many have chosen to be an instrument of wickedness used by the Devil to perform the works of darkness. But the Apostle Paul encourages us in Romans 13:12b (TLV), *"Let us put off the works of darkness and put on the armor of light."*

Notice that the teenage boy in my dream changed his mind and chose not to be an instrument of darkness. Each of us have this same choice: to do good or to do evil. We must understand that our decision comes with a heavy weight of responsibility. One night, the Lord began to show me something interesting in Matthew 27. In this chapter, Judas, who was one of Jesus' Apostles, willingly aligned himself with the Devil (also called Satan) to betray Jesus. Let's look at Mark 14:10-11 (NIV) to see what Judas did. *"Then Judas Iscariot, one of the Twelve, went to the chief priests to betray Jesus to them. They were delighted to hear this and promised to give him money. So he [Judas] watched for an opportunity to hand Him [Jesus] over."*

Then, in Luke 22:3 (NIV) we read that Judas not only came into agreement with the evil chief priests, but that as Passover was approaching, ***"Satan entered Judas."*** During this supper, Jesus exposes Judas as the betrayer, and Judas leaves and returns later with the soldiers to arrest Jesus. Jesus was brought before the chief priests and questioned and then was condemned to death.

Matthew 27:3-5 (NIV) continues: *"When Judas, who had betrayed him, saw that Jesus was condemned, he was seized with remorse and returned the thirty pieces of silver to the chief priests and the elder. 'I have sinned,' he said, 'for I have betrayed innocent blood.' 'What is that to us?' they replied.* ***'That's your responsibility.'*** *So Judas threw the money into the temple and left. Then he went away and hanged himself."* The Apostle Paul explains:

> *"You cannot drink the cup of the Lord and the cup of demons too; you cannot have a part in both the Lord's table and the table of demons."*
> 2 Corinthians 10:21, NIV

Sadly, Judas quickly learned that he could not drink from both the cup of the Lord and the cup of demons. Then, shortly thereafter in Matthew 27:22 (NIV), Jesus is standing before Pilate, and Pilate asks the crowd what crime Jesus committed. But the crowd could give no answer and only shouted, *"Crucify Him!"* Verse 24-25 (NIV) continues: *"When Pilate saw that he was getting nowhere, but that instead an uproar was starting, he took water and washed his hands in front of the crowd. 'I am innocent of this man's blood,' he said. '**It is your responsibility!**' All the people answered, 'Let His blood be on us and on our children!'"* We must be very careful who we choose to align ourselves with because, ultimately, **the path we choose is our responsibility**.

CHOOSE TO BE AN INSTRUMENT OF RIGHTEOUSNESS

After Jesus was baptized by his cousin John, He went to the desert where He fasted for forty days. During this time, Jesus was tempted by the Devil, but he chose to reject the Devil's offers and fulfill His mission with God. Like Jesus, we have a choice to make. We can agree with the Devil, or we can choose to be an instrument of God operating in His righteousness on Earth (Romans 6:13).

Again, our specific action steps are to choose Jesus Christ as our Lord and Savior. With His righteousness operating in us, and as we continue in the Word of God and follow the Spirit, we are choosing to live a prayerful (asking) and fasted (obeying) lifestyle. As discussed, fasting is to abstain from food or drink for spiritual purposes. To live a fasted lifestyle is to choose to humbly obey God. Yet we read of another fast that is pleasing to God in Isaiah 58 where God tells the people they are to help and care for others.

> *"Is not this the kind of fasting I have chosen: to loose the chains of injustice and untie the cords of the yoke, to set the oppressed free and break every yoke? Is it not to share your food with the hungry and to provide the poor wanderer with shelter when you see the naked,*

*to clothe them, and not to turn away from your own
flesh and blood? Then your light will break forth like
the dawn, and your healing will quickly appear; then
your righteousness will go before you, and the glory of
the Lord will be your rear guard. Then you will call,
and the Lord will answer; you will cry for help, and
He will say: Here am I."*
Isaiah 58:6-9, NIV

Under the New Covenant, we cannot be saved by what we do, and we could never be good enough to be in right standing with God. It is only through Jesus Christ that our sins may be forgiven and taken away so we may come into a relationship with the Father God and be given eternal life. As we come to know Jesus and the Father God and Their great love for us, our heart is changed, and we will begin to express our faith through loving God and loving others. The Apostle Paul wrote, *"What is important is faith expressing itself in LOVE"* (Galatians 5:6, NLT).

What kind of love is this that makes us want to care for others?

[1] Knight and Ray, *Layman's,* 136-137.

[2] Milligan, *Understanding the Dreams You Dream,* 246.

[3] G3794 - ochyroma - *Strong's Greek Lexicon* (kjv) Blue Letter Bible. Accessed 5 Mar, 2025. https://www.blueletterbible.org/lexicon/g3794/kjv/tr/0-1/

[4] Gordon Robertson, The Christian Broadcasting Network, *"700 Club, October 12, 2011,"* video, 38:10, Accessed Mar 5, 2025. https://www2.cbn.com/video/700-club/700-club-october-12-2011.

[5] H1176 - Baalzebub - *Strong's Hebrew Lexicon* (kjv) Blue Letter Bible. Accessed Mar 5, 2025. https://www.blueletterbible.org/lexicon/h1176/kjv/wlc/0-1/

[6] Richards, *Expository,* 265.

[7] Knight and Ray, *Layman's,* 318.

[8] Terry Moore, *The Cross is the Key* (Legacy Press, Carrollton, TX, 2021), 23-63.

[9] Terry Moore, *Love, Identity, and Purpose* (Legacy Press, Carrollton, TX, 2021), 29-39.

[10] *Webster's New World Dictionary of the American Language,* Warner Books Paperback Edition (Simon & Schuster, New York, NY, 1982), 126.

Chapter Five

WE HELP OTHERS TAKE THEIR DEBT AWAY

In my college days, I had a hall mate who began sharing some Scriptures from her Bible with me. I was so surprised that she knew exactly where to find all the answers to my questions. She said she had learned the Bible from a very young age and knew it well. I remember being so impressed by this and that she had the boldness to approach me.

This hall mate was planting seeds in my life that would later bloom. She and so many others God put in my path were helping me to recognize my need for Him. I came to have a deeper passion for the Lord because of their loving influence. Now, I want to do the same. I can't imagine living my life without God, His Son Jesus, and the help of the Holy Spirit. I want to share the Lord Jesus Christ with others so their sin debt will be taken away and so they can learn to live a more abundant life.

Jesus said before He ascended to Heaven, "*All authority in heaven and on earth has been given to Me. Go therefore and make disciples of all nations, immersing them in the name of the Father and the Son and the Holy Spirit, teaching them to observe all I have commanded you. And remember! I am with you always, even to the end of the age*" (Matthew 28:18-20, TLV). We see that the Apostle Paul dearly loved Jesus and was passionate about telling others about Him. Paul encourages us to do the same and wrote, "*We should help others do what is right and build them up in the Lord*" (Romans 15:2, NLT).

So how can we, as believers, help others come to know Jesus Christ? The Apostle Paul writes the following:

"... be kind to each other, tenderhearted, forgiving one another, just as God through Christ has forgiven you. Follow God's example in everything you do, because you are His dear children. Live a life filled with love for others, following the example of Christ, who loved you and gave Himself as a sacrifice to take away your sins. And God was pleased, because that sacrifice was like sweet perfume to Him."
Ephesians 4:32 and 5:1 NLT

The NIV version reads: ***"Be kind and compassionate to one another, forgiving each other, just as in Christ God forgave you.*** *Be imitators of God, therefore, as dearly loved children and live a life of love, just as Christ loved us and gave Himself up for us as a fragrant offering and sacrifice to God."* Let's take a closer look at this Scripture.

BE KIND AND COMPASSIONATE TO ONE ANOTHER

In Scripture, Jesus was kind and had compassion for others. *"When Jesus went ashore, He saw a large crowd [waiting], and He was moved with compassion for them because they were like sheep without a shepherd [lacking guidance]; and He began to teach them many things"* (Mark 6:34, AMP). Another example of Jesus' compassion was when He showed kindness to two blind men. *"Jesus had compassion on them and touched their eyes. Immediately they received their sight and followed Him"* (Matthew 20:34, NIV). We see Jesus also showed kindness to a man with leprosy. *"Moved with compassion [for his suffering], Jesus reached out with His hand and touched him, and said to him, 'I am willing; be cleansed.' The leprosy left him immediately and he was cleansed [completely healed and restored*

118

to health]" (Mark 1:41-42, AMP). Notice in these examples that Jesus followed compassion with action. According to Proverbs 25:11, kindness toward others can be as simple as a kind word spoken at the appropriate time. But no matter how big or small, Galatians 6:10 encourages us to do good things and think of ways to bless others. We should be mindful of ways we can be useful, helpful, and kind to one another.

Sadly, some people are blind to the needs of others, but as believers, God intends for us to be compassionate and comfort others. The Apostle Paul wrote, *"God is our merciful Father and the source of all comfort. He comforts us in all our troubles so we can comfort others. When they are troubled, we will be able to give them the same comfort God has given us"* (2 Corinthians 1:3b-4, NLT). Jesus gives us a parable as an example in Luke 10:30-37, the story of the Good Samaritan. A man was beaten and robbed, and the thieves left him on the road from Jerusalem to Jericho. A priest and a Levite chose to pass him by, but the Samaritan had compassion on him and bandaged his wounds, brought him to an inn, and paid for his stay. Jesus goes on to say, *"Go, and you do the same"* (Luke 10:37, TLV). Interestingly, it was the Samaritan who helped the injured man. In those days, Samaritans were viewed by the Jews as a lower class of people, and perhaps this Samaritan had less money than the others who passed him by, yet he was the one who had compassion and took action to help the stranger in need.

Notice as well that the Samaritan man spent his own money to help this injured man. The Bible mentions giving away money, called "tithes and offerings." The word tithe means a giving of one-tenth portion.[1] The word *offerings* can mean aid, contributions, gifts, donations, help, or assistance.

(Tithes and offerings are mentioned in the following Scriptures: Malachi 3:8-12; Deuteronomy 14:22-29; Nehemiah 10:37-39; Matthew 23:23.)

Another important aspect of helping others is to pray. Praying for others gives us compassion for people. When we have compassion for people, we want to help them come to know a caring God who loves them dearly. I dreamt years ago I had the HIV-AIDS virus. At that time, the disease was not well understood, and in my dream, I was consumed with feelings of rejection, isolation, and fear. This dream caused me to have compassion for people with AIDS and to pray for them. The Apostle Peter encourages us to *"be harmonious, sympathetic, brotherly, tenderhearted, humble minded"* (1 Peter 3:8, TLV).

As the years passed, the Lord instructed me to pray for more and more people. One night I dreamt I was to get a small box and index cards. On the index cards, I was to write the names of people the Lord would bring to my mind, and this would help me to remember to pray for them. The Apostle Paul wrote, *"Devote yourselves to prayer with an alert mind and a thankful heart"* (Colossians 4:2, NLT). As I did this, God began to show me specific ways to pray for people. For example, the Lord impressed me to pray for a married couple I had known many years ago. The Lord showed me specifically that the wife had lost her love for her husband because of his selfishness. I did not expose this information, but because of my dream, I knew exactly how to pray for this couple.

If we are unsure what to pray, Jesus tells us how to pray in Matthew 6:

> *"When you pray, go into your room, close the door and pray to your Father, who is unseen. Then your Father, who sees what is done in secret, will reward you. And when you pray, do not keep on babbling like pagans, for they think*

they will be heard because of their many words. Do not be like them, for your Father knows what you need before you ask Him. This, then, is how you should pray:

'Our Father in heaven, hallowed be your name, your kingdom come, your will be done, on earth as it is in heaven. Give us today our daily bread. And forgive us our debts, as we also have forgiven our debtors. And lead us not into temptation, but deliver us from the evil one.' For if you forgive men when they sin against you, your heavenly Father will also forgive you."

Matthew 6:6-14, NIV

FORGIVE EACH OTHER JUST AS IN CHRIST GOD FORGAVE YOU

Forgiveness must be important to God because it is mentioned several times in the above passage. The forgiveness of our sins through Jesus Christ is the ultimate and greatest example of forgiveness. While hanging on the cross, Jesus prayed, *"Father, forgive them, for they do not know what they are doing"* (Luke 23:34, NIV). (Also read Matthew 27 and 28; Mark 15 and 16.) As impossible as it seems, Jesus also forgave those who so brutally tortured and horrifically crucified Him on the cross. God freely gives us the gift of forgiveness through Jesus, and now He instructs us also to forgive others.

What does forgiveness have to do with helping others? Forgiving others gives people a glimpse of being forgiven by the Father in Heaven for all their sins. That said, forgiveness does not mean the offender is not responsible to God for their actions. God sees all things, and everyone will be held accountable for any unforgiven (unrepented) offense (Colossians 3:25). Forgiveness is defined as "to pardon, remission of a penalty ..."[2] As in Jesus' case, to forgive a debt. Unforgiveness is *not* to forgive; that is to retain a debt. Like keeping our sin debt, unforgiveness can internalize, causing us pain and torment.

Years ago, I had a friend who had very serious health challenges and was struggling in her marriage. The Lord gave me a dream and showed me my friend had made a list of all the bad things her husband had ever said and done. In my dream, I saw her walking up and down the pharmacy aisle, repeating these offenses over and over like a broken record. Because her mind was stuck in this endless loop, resentment and bitterness began to take root, and it was making her sick. Hebrews 12:15 (NIV) warns us, *"See to it that no one misses the grace of God and that no bitter root grows up to cause trouble and defile many."* This is why we must not internalize our offenses but release them to God through forgiveness so we may live in peace.

One night, the Lord gave me spiritual insight concerning someone dealing with the disappointment of a failed business. In this dream, I could see flesh wounds on this person's left arm, and these slashes were very deep and bloody. I heard the Lord say, "His wounds have turned to bitterness." In this dream, the Lord showed me that this man had worked very hard to make his business successful, but it failed. Now, it was time to put his efforts into something else. Our wounds (hurts, offenses, and disappointments in life) can turn to bitterness, or they can be healed through forgiveness and trusting God to work all things for our good. Romans 8:28 (NLT) tells us, *"And we know that God causes everything to work together for the good of those who love God and are called according to His purpose for them."*

All bitterness needs to be emptied out so we can become the vessel God wants us to be. Interestingly, the first part of Ephesians 4 reads: ***"Let all bitterness and indignation and*** *wrath and resentment (anger, animosity) and quarreling and slander (evil speaking, abusive or blasphemous language) be banished from you, with all malice (spite, ill will, or baseness of any kind).* *And become useful and helpful and kind to one another, tenderhearted, forgiving one another, as God in Christ forgave you"* (Ephesians 4:31-32, AMP). If we allow these bad feelings to remain inside of us, they can build up as hatred and explode out to other people as anger.

One night, I had a dream in which the Lord showed me I was harboring anger about some things in my past. I woke up thinking, "I didn't know I had any anger!" A few nights later the Lord said I needed "Spiritual Surgery." You may remember that in the armor of God, the sword of the Spirit is the Word of God. Recall, *"For the word of God is full of living power.* **It is sharper than the sharpest knife, cutting deep into our innermost thoughts and desires"** (Hebrews 4:12, NLT). The Word of God is the tool we use, along with the revelation of the Spirit, to have Spiritual Surgery. So, I began researching what the Word of God had to say about anger. I came to see that my anger issue was related to forgiving others. James 1:19b-21, NIV reads, *"… for man's anger does not bring about the righteous life that God desires … humbly accept the word planted in you, which can save you."* Jesus is the Seed planted in us. As He grows in us through the watering of the Word of God (the Bible) and with the help of the Holy Spirit, we can forgive and cut away the hurts and disappointments of our past.

A few nights after this first dream, God showed me specific people He wanted me to forgive and the exact offense for each of them. I was shocked at the detail given for each offense. Because God was so specific, I realized He saw every aspect of my life and cared for me deeply, and this helped me to forgive.

It is to our benefit to forgive. Even though we may feel our circumstances are unjust and unfair, we are still responsible for how we respond to the offenses laid against us. God is good, and He will help us to forgive, as we see in the example of Joseph in the Bible.

JOSEPH CHOSE TO FORGIVE

Joseph was the son of Jacob, later called Israel. His story is found in Genesis 36-50. *"Now Israel [Jacob] loved Joseph more than all his children"* (Genesis 37:3, AMP). Because of this, the other children were jealous and hated Joseph. In fact, they hated him so much that they could not speak peaceably to him. Joseph had two dreams of being elevated and put in a place of honor and power. Upon telling his family his dreams, his brothers hated him even more. One day, the brothers acted out their hatred by kidnapping Joseph and selling him into slavery. Joseph was further falsely accused and unjustly imprisoned. In all, he suffered about thirteen or fourteen years of bondage. Joseph had much to be angry about, but through these troubles, the Bible says, *"The Lord was with Joseph, and he [even though a slave] became a successful and prosperous man"* (Genesis 39:2, AMP). God delivered and even promoted Joseph to a position of great authority in all of Egypt. When famine hit the land, the brothers of Joseph traveled to Egypt for food. They stood before him requesting provisions without recognizing him. Joseph had a choice to make. He could take his revenge or forgive his brothers and end the cycle of hatred. Joseph chose to forgive and said to his brothers, *"'Please come closer to me.' And they approached him. And he said, 'I am Joseph your brother, whom you sold into Egypt. Now do not be distressed or angry with yourselves because you sold me here, for God sent me ahead of you to save life and preserve our family'"* (Genesis 45:4-6, AMP). What a sense of purpose Joseph had! He forgave! Forgiveness cleared his heart and mind which helped him to focus on his destiny.

Interestingly, Joseph tells his brothers not to be angry with themselves. The Apostle Paul wrote, *"If your enemy is hungry, feed him; if he is thirsty, give him something to drink. In doing this, you will heap burning coals on his head"* (Romans 12:19-21, NIV). Joseph did exactly that. Not only did Joseph forgive them, but he chose to feed the very brothers who sold him into slavery. Further, he blessed them by giving his family the prime land in all of Egypt (Genesis 45:7-8). We can only imagine how his brothers felt about the forgiveness and kindness extended to them by Joseph. It must have melted their hardened hearts.

Jesus tells us in Luke 6:35-36 (NLT), *"Love your enemies! Do good to them. Lend to them without expecting to be repaid. Then your reward from heaven will be very great, and you will truly be acting as children of the Most High, for he is kind to those who are unthankful and wicked. You must be compassionate, just as your Father is compassionate."* God did reward Joseph. The names of Joseph's two sons are very interesting. *"Joseph named his firstborn Manasseh and said, 'It is because God has made me forget all my trouble and all my father's household.' The second son he named Ephraim and said, 'It is because God has made me fruitful in the land of my suffering'"* (Genesis 41:51-52, NIV). Joseph chose to forgive, and God gave Joseph the ability to forget his past and become fruitful.

What an amazing example of forgiveness and mercy! Joseph remained faithful to God through his trials, hanging on to the dreams he had received from God so many years before. Then, in God's perfect timing, he was raised up and put in a place of honor and power.

Just as Joseph was innocent yet hated by his brothers, Jesus was also innocent and hated by the chief priests, elders, and teachers of the law, which was also a result of jealousy and envy (Matthew 27). Jesus, being our perfect example here on Earth, forgave all who put Him on the cross, and the Father seated Him at His right side in the Kingdom of Heaven. Both Joseph and Jesus chose to forgive, and for doing so, they were both greatly rewarded.

It doesn't make sense that Jesus or Joseph forgave. In many cases, it simply does not make sense for us to forgive either, but we need to trust God that forgiveness is the path to supernatural freedom from all offenses. If we turn to God, God will change our hearts in ways beyond our human comprehension and give us peace.

OTHERS HAVE CHOSEN TO FORGIVE

A current-day example of forgiveness can be seen in the life of Gracia Burnham. Gracia showed a divine ability to forgive. She and her husband were missionaries in the Philippines, where they were kidnapped and held for ransom. It was a difficult ordeal, and Christians around the world were praying for their release. Gracia survived, but her husband did not. He was killed by gunfire when the government closed in on their captors. When interviewed, Gracia said she *forgave*

126

those men who had caused her such great pain and her husband's death.[3] By choosing to forgive, Gracia ended the cycle of hatred.

FORGIVENESS ENDS THE CYCLE OF HATRED

It is human nature to harbor hatred and unforgiveness. In our human spirit, we *"were foolish, disobedient, deceived and enslaved by all kinds of passions and pleasures. We lived in malice and envy, being hated and hating one another"* (Titus 3:3, NKJV). Operating in our human spirit is operating independently from God. But it is God's desire that we forgive. He helps us to forgive through the Holy Spirit. In 2 Timothy 1:7 (AMP), it tells us, *"For God did not give us a spirit of timidity or cowardice or fear, but [He has given us a spirit] of power and of love and of sound judgment and personal discipline [abilities that result in a calm, well-balanced mind and self-control]."* With the Holy Spirit operating in us, we have the power to forgive, the ability to love purely from the heart, and the self-discipline to keep our thoughts on God, which will give us a sound mind and peace.

If we still struggle to forgive, we can do as Jesus said in one of His sermons, *"Love your enemies and **pray** for those who persecute you"* (Matthew 5:44, NIV). Jesus is not telling us to keep our enemies ever-present on our minds, but when they do come to mind, we can pray and allow God to step in and do a work within us rather than giving that place to the Devil to torment our minds.

On one occasion, I was really struggling to forgive a person of authority who had treated someone close to me very unfairly. The Lord gave me two dreams. In the first dream, the Lord gave me insight into this person's mind. I saw the tremendous mental torment this person was experiencing. I literally saw two demons pounding his head into the concrete; he was that tortured. In the second dream, this person asked me, "Do you pray?"

I said, "Yes, I pray."

He asked, "Will you pray for me?"

I said, "Yes, I will."

I awoke with a new understanding of the importance of prayer and the above Scripture instructing us to pray for those who persecute you.

Now, when I think about this person, I pray for him. With time, my anger was dissolved. Remember, Jesus prayed and asked the Father to forgive those who had just brutally tortured Him and hung Him on the cross. He was showing us the way to true freedom.

FORGIVING OTHERS SHOWS THE WORLD WE ARE A CHILD OF GOD

The above Scripture continues, *"I tell you, love your enemies and pray for those who persecute you, **to show** that you are the children of the Father Who is in heaven; for He makes His sun rise on the wicked and on the good, and makes the rain fall upon the upright and the wrongdoers. For if you love those who love you, what reward can you have?"* (Matthew 5:44-46, AMP). Our forgiving others is what sets us apart as Christians, and as mentioned earlier, it gives people a glimpse of being forgiven by the Father in Heaven for all of their sins.

Many people have lived through some really horrible things. Whether our offenders pay in this world or not, we must give our offense to God and let God deal with the judgment. I remember at a young age hearing stories about the holocaust and watching old videos of the surviving victims. I recall one woman whose family members were murdered, and she was treated brutally. She said that when she cried out to God, she felt His love come over her, which then gave her the supernatural ability to forgive her offenders. Psalm 34:15 (NKJV) promises, *"The eyes of the Lord are on the righteous, And His ears are open to their cry."* This woman chose to focus on God and was comforted by the Holy Spirit so she could forgive and go on to live in peace.

Apostle Paul said we are to forgive *"in order that Satan might not outwit us. For we are not unaware of his schemes"* (2 Corinthians 2:11, NIV). If we do not forgive, Satan has outwitted us and has an entryway to torment us, as my next dream shows. In this dream, I saw three open windows. Each window was open at a different level; one was open wide, and the other two were just a crack. But no matter how small the crack, the Lord showed me that the enemy can get in! We need to fully close ALL the windows to be fully protected, and we do this by choosing to forgive all offenses. This is what Jesus did: He said the prince of this world was coming, but *"he has no hold over Me"* (John 14:30, NIV). Satan had no entryway to attack Jesus.[4] Likewise, we need complete closure of all entryways!

We must not let Satan outwit us, giving him access to torment us with internalized pain, hatred, and anger. Instead, we must forgive by turning to God through prayer, asking for God's help, diving into the Word of God, and through the power of the Holy Spirit helping us and operating in us. When we forgive, we align ourselves with the Father God and His perfect plan for our life.

WE MUST FORGIVE SO THAT WE MAY BE FORGIVEN

The importance of forgiveness is explained by Jesus in a parable in Matthew 18:22-35 (NLT). The story is about a servant who was in financial debt to the king. The amount was so great that he was unable to pay. The servant begged for forgiveness. *"The lord of the servant was moved with compassion and loosed him and forgave him the debt."* Then, the servant went out and found one of his fellow servants who owed him and demanded, *"Pay back what you owe me."* He even had the man thrown into prison until he could repay the debt. The master (hearing what had happened) called the servant in. *"You wicked servant,"* he said, *"I canceled all that debt of yours, because you begged me to. Shouldn't you have had mercy on your fellow servant just as I had on you?"* In anger, his master turned him over to the jailers to be tortured until he could pay back all he owed. Jesus said, *"This is how my heavenly Father will treat each of you unless you forgive your brother from your heart."* Mark 11:25 (NIV) further encourages us, *"When you stand praying, if you hold anything against anyone, forgive him, so that your Father in heaven may forgive you your sins."*

The man in the above story forgot the mercy shown him and the enormous debt forgiven him; therefore, he was unforgiving of others. This parable tells us we must **remember the sacrifice Jesus made for each of us on the cross, and when we do,** we will be able to extend mercy and forgiveness to others. The Apostle Paul states:

> *"Since God chose you to be the holy people whom he loves, you must clothe yourselves with tenderhearted mercy, kindness, humility, gentleness, and patience. You must make allowance for each other's faults and forgive the person who offends you.* **Remember, the Lord forgave you, so you must forgive others.** *And the*

most important piece of clothing you must wear is love.
Love is what binds us all together in perfect harmony."
Colossians 3:12-14, NLT

One of my favorite stories in the Bible is in Luke 7. In this story, a woman in the city was a *"notorious sinner"* (Luke 7:39, AMP). When this woman heard Jesus was at a Jewish Pharisee's house, she brought some perfumed ointment and went to the house. Standing behind Jesus, she affectionately kissed and washed His feet with her tears and wiped them with her hair. She anointed Him with oil. The host was shocked to see such a display, thinking that if Jesus was a prophet, He would not let this woman touch Him. But Jesus saw her heart. He saw that she had received His love, and this caused her not to consider herself or her past or care about what others thought of her.

Knowing the disapproval of those watching her, Jesus explained her extravagant expression of love in a parable. *"Two men owed money to a certain moneylender. One owed him five hundred denarii and the other fifty. Neither of them had the money to pay him back, so he forgave the debts of both. Now which of them will love him more?' Simon replied, 'I suppose the one who had the bigger debt forgiven.' 'You have judged correctly' Jesus said"* (Luke 7:41-43, NIV). Jesus went on to say in verse 47, *"Therefore, I tell you, her many sins have been forgiven —as her great love has shown. But whoever has been forgiven little loves little."* The New Living Translation reads, *"I tell you, her sins—and they are many—have been forgiven, so she has shown Me much love. But a person who is forgiven little shows only little love"* (Luke 7:47, NLT).

This woman was drawn to Jesus because she was able to fully grasp that though she had sin in her life, she was deeply loved. This love so overwhelmed her that she was not focused on herself or her sin but on Jesus. Each of us must come to this same recognition and understanding—that we are so very dearly loved.

*"God showed how much He loved us by sending His one
and only Son into the world so that we might have eternal
life through Him. This is real love—not that we loved
God, but that He loved us and sent His Son as a
sacrifice to take away our sins."*
1 John 4:9-10, NLT

Knowing we are dearly loved means so much and changes our entire outlook on life. Several years ago, I felt God's love when I had just awoken from having a major surgery. I have had many surgeries, and this had never happened to me before. But this time, upon waking from the surgery, I could feel God's overwhelming presence come upon me. It felt like He was filling me with His love. It felt like He was holding and embracing me into His very being. When we know this amazing love of the Father God and the love of Jesus—that we are so dearly loved—it is overwhelming (in a good way!) and completely consuming.

The Apostle Paul wrote in his letter to the Ephesians about the importance of fully embracing God's love for us by praying, *"I pray that you, being rooted and established in love, may have power, together with all the saints, to grasp how wide and long and high and deep is the love of Christ, and* **to know this love** *that surpasses knowledge—that you may* **be filled to the measure of all the fullness of God"** (Ephesians 3:17b-19, NIV). God made Jesus the link between us and Himself; therefore, the process of being filled with the fullness of God's love begins with our faith in Jesus Christ. Our faith in Jesus is the foundation that takes us step by step to living a life of love.

"For this very reason, make every effort to
add to your faith *goodness;
and to goodness, knowledge;*

and to knowledge, self-control;
and to self-control, perseverance;
and to perseverance, godliness;
and to godliness, brotherly kindness;
*and to brotherly kindness, **love**."*
2 Peter 1:5-7, NIV

Notice that this process starts with faith and ends with love. This may be why the Apostle Paul wrote to the Galatians that what matters is faith expressing itself through love (Galatians 5:6). This is our faith in Jesus Christ growing full bloom into love. Peter goes on to reiterate we can get to this place of love by knowing the depth of God's love for us.

"For if you possess these qualities [goodness, knowledge,
self-control, perseverance, godliness, brotherly kindness,
and love] in increasing measure, they will keep you from
being ineffective and unproductive in your knowledge of
our Lord Jesus Christ. But if anyone does not have
*them, he is nearsighted and blind, and **has forgotten***
that he has been cleansed from his past sins.
Therefore, my brothers, be all the more eager to make
your calling and election sure. For if you do these things,
you will never fall, and you will receive a rich
welcome into the eternal kingdom of our
Lord and Savior Jesus Christ."
2 Peter 1:8-13, NIV

Keeping this knowledge (that we are forgiven through Jesus and are so dearly loved) ever-present in our minds and in our hearts helps us increase to the full measure of love. Just as hatred can overflow to others as anger, love will overflow to others when we are faith-filled (1 Thessalonians 3:12). In 1 Corinthians 13:4-7 and 13 (NKJV) we can know what love is and is not:

*"Love suffers long and is kind; love does not envy; love
does not parade itself, is not puffed up; does not behave
rudely, does not seek its own, is not provoked, thinks
no evil; does not rejoice in iniquity, but rejoices in the
truth; bears all things, believes all things, hopes all
things, endures all things. Love never fails…And now
abide faith, hope, love, these three;
but the greatest of these is love."*

When I read these words, I thought, "How can anyone love like this?" Interestingly, I found that Young's Literal Translation of this Scripture uses the definite article (defines the noun it modifies) of the word "the." It reads, *"The love … is kind,"* … *"The love doth never fail."* The love refers to God's love. Because God is love, with *The* love (of God) in us, we can love others.

How do we get the love of God in us? The Apostle Paul writes, *"For we know how dearly God loves us because He has given us the Holy Spirit to fill our hearts with His love"* (Romans 5:5b, NLT). If we struggle with loving people (as most of us do!), we can start by praying, "Lord, I ask that Your Holy Spirit fill my heart with Your love." With God's love in us, we can love others.

This is how Jesus did it—He had God's love in Him. He showed His love for others by having compassion for the lost, healing the sick, delivering the oppressed, feeding the poor, and teaching others about the Father God. In 1 John 2:5b-6 (NIV), it tells us, *"This is how we know we are in Him: Whoever claims to live in Him must live as Jesus did."* This is a tall order, but after His resurrection, Jesus appeared to the Apostle Peter and challenged him to show his love for others. John 21:15-17 (NIV) records their conversation:

"Jesus said to Simon Peter, 'Simon son of John, do you truly love me more than these?' 'Yes, Lord,' he said, 'you

know that I love you.' Jesus said, 'Feed my lambs.'
Again Jesus said, 'Simon son of John, do you truly love
me?' He answered, 'Yes, Lord, you know that I love
you.' Jesus said, 'Take care of my sheep.' The third time
he said to him, 'Simon son of John, do you love me?'
Peter was hurt because Jesus asked him the third time.
'Do you love me?' He said, 'Lord, you know all things;
you know that I love you.' Jesus said, 'Feed my sheep.'"

After all that Peter had witnessed in watching Jesus die on the cross, Peter knew Jesus deeply loved him. Knowing how dearly we are loved creates a desire to love God with everything in us. Jesus was asked, *"What is the most important commandment?"* He answered, *"Love the Lord your God with all your heart and with all your soul and with all your mind and with all your strength. The second is this: Love your neighbor as yourself. There is no commandment greater than these"* (Mark 12:28, 30-31, NIV). Notice that love is common in both commandments.

Jesus also said, *"A new commandment I give you: Love one another. As I have loved you, so you must love one another. By this all men will know that you are my disciples, if you love one another"* (John 13:34-35, NIV). Please take a moment also to read 1 John 4: 11-21. The Apostle Paul in Romans 13:9b-10 (NIV) simplifies love in this way, *"'Love your neighbor as yourself.' Love does no harm to a neighbor. Therefore, love is the fulfillment of the law."*

Now, back to the above conversation between Jesus and Peter, Jesus was telling Peter that if His love was truly in him, he should show this love to others. Jesus cared so passionately for people and stated that when we give food and drink to the needy, clothe the poor, help the sick, and visit those in prison, it is as though we are doing it for Him (Matthew 25:35-40). And this takes us to the last part of Ephesians 4:32-5:1 (NIV). *"Be kind and compassionate (tender-*

hearted) to one another, forgiving each other, just as in Christ God forgave you. **Be imitators (followers) of God, therefore, as dearly loved children and live a life of love, just as Christ loved us and gave Himself up for us as a fragrant offering and sacrifice to God."**

Jesus lived a life of love through serving others. *"For even the Son of Man came not to be served but to serve others and to give his life as a ransom for many"* (Mark 10:45, NLT). As Jesus was God's gift to the world, the Apostle Paul wrote in his letter to the Romans that we are to use our many different gifts to serve others:

> *"Therefore, I urge you, brothers, in view of God's mercy,*
> *to offer your bodies as living sacrifices, holy and pleasing to*
> *God—this is your spiritual act of worship. . . . We have*
> *different gifts, according to the grace given us.*
> *If a man's gift is prophesying, let him use it in proportion*
> *to his faith. If it is serving, let him serve; if it is teaching,*
> *let him teach; if it is encouraging, let him encourage;*
> *if it is contributing to the needs of others, let him give*
> *generously; if it is leadership, let him govern diligently;*
> *if it is showing mercy, let him do it cheerfully."*
> Romans 12:1 & 6-8, NIV

When we use our giftings (talents and skills) to serve others, we please God and bless others. The Apostle Peter encourages us: *"Each one should use whatever gift he has received to serve others, faithfully administering God's grace in its various forms"* (1 Peter 4:10, NIV).

People spend years upon years trying to find their way and meaning in life. Unfortunately, many of us look for joy and fulfillment in empty places. I saw a teen boy on a TV show say that he was entering a contest because, "He was tired of working." He was so young and already tired of

136

working! If this boy only knew he could ask God for direction in his life, and if he acted on that plan, it would bring him great joy and fulfillment.

If you don't know what your giftings are, *ask* God to show you. God's plan for our lives is far more abundant than we can ever hope to dream of for ourselves. And all we have to do is ASK. *"Call to me, and I will answer you and tell you great and unsearchable things you do not know"* (Jeremiah 33:3, NIV). It is just that simple. One night, I was lying in bed thinking that all my friends seemed to have such amazing giftings and goals they were pursuing. Sadly, I felt like I had no apparent direction. I asked the Lord what He had for me, and that night, He showed me my future and what He had for me to do. It was exciting to hear from the Lord, to know that He had a plan just for me, and this blessed me so very much.

God has a plan and a purpose for each of us. *"For we are God's workmanship, created in Christ Jesus to do good works, which God prepared in advance for us to do"* (Ephesians 2:10, NIV). NLT reads, *"For we are God's masterpiece."* I love that!

We can each be a part of God's amazing plan; all we have to do is ask through prayer and then obey as directed. I was given a dream where I was told to "pray more." I woke up thinking, "Well, I can do that." Then that very next night, I had another dream. In this dream, I was busy doing volunteer work, which I thought was good (and it is good), but in my dream, the Lord spoke very sternly to me, "WHY are you working?" His words startled me. God was serious! He wanted me to pray FIRST, get His direction and then move forward with His plan. Just because volunteering is good, I should not have assumed it was God! It is through prayer that we come to *know* God's will so that we can then do His will.

Psalm 85:13 (NIV) states, *"Righteousness goes before him and prepares the way for his steps."*

As we walk with Jesus and live in His righteousness through being both prayerful (asking) and fasted (obeying), we come to learn what God wants us to do and how He wants us to love others. Deuteronomy 11:22b (NLT) states, *"Show love to the Lord your God by walking in His ways and holding tightly to Him."*

After these dreams, I was given another dream illustrating the importance of this order: to pray and then obey. In this dream, I was driving a large bus, and there also appeared to be trailer attachments behind the bus. (The trailer attachments represented people who were following me.) Interestingly, rather than the driver's seat being at the front of the bus, the driver's seat was at the back. With the steering wheel in the back of the bus, it was virtually impossible to see anything down the road. I was trying to drive this bus (with others following me), and I had absolutely no idea where I was going. The Lord was showing me that I was going and doing before I knew what He wanted me to do. As a result, I was going astray and taking other people with me!

This is why prayer is so important. It allows us to first gain a vision of our mission so we know how to obey. Otherwise, we are aimlessly—sometimes recklessly—putting all our effort, energy, money, and time into something that is not the will of God. Our mission and strategy must be God-directed. We receive this direction through prayer.

GOD SHOWS US THE WAY, BUT IT IS UP TO US TO OBEY

Whether it is for our career or volunteer work, we should ask what God wants us to do and then obey! We can live fulfilled and blessed lives by asking what God has for us and then doing as He directs. *"Commit your work to the Lord, and then your plans will succeed"* (Proverbs 16:3, NLT). Commit means we are all in! We want to pray for God's plan and ask for His strategy and wisdom so we can then take action and fully commit!

Bruce Wilkinson, author of the number one *New York Times* bestseller *The Prayer of Jabez: Breaking Through to the Blessed Life* and *Secrets of the Vine: Breaking Through to Abundance* books, obeyed the call of God to teach poor African families how to grow small gardens so that they could feed their families. Dr. Wilkinson was faithful and had a personal goal to provide the seed, training, and harvesting of food for one million individual African families. Now, that is exciting![5]

Suppose God gives you a dream or a vision for something He wants you to do, and you are excited about it, but then you think, "This seems impossible; how can this be done?" Jesus did what seemed impossible when, on two occasions, He fed the multitudes. Jesus fed 5,000 (plus women and children) in Matthew 14:13-21, and 4,000 (plus women and children) in Matthew 15:29-39 and Luke 9:13. Jesus used what resources were available—a few loaves of bread and fish— He prayed, they obeyed His instructions, and God provided the miracle.

AMAZING THINGS CAN BE ACCOMPLISHED WHEN WE PRAYERFULLY ASK AND OBEY

I love the story of Richard Proudfit. He had gone to Honduras after a devastating hurricane to help restore the country and witnessed widespread starvation. He said he heard God's call: "If you've seen my starving children, go and feed them." "This call would become both the name and the mission of Feed My Starving Children." Because of Mr. Proudfit's passion for helping others and his obedience to act, God worked mightily through this man to develop a nutritional meal pack that feeds millions of starving children in many countries around the world.[6]

Operating in our God-given gifting goes beyond being kind, helpful, and useful to others because it is a giving of ourselves. *"Do not neglect your gift ... Be diligent in these matters; give yourself wholly to them, so that everyone may see your progress"* (1 Timothy 4:14, NIV). It pleases God when we use our giftings, in obedience to His will, to help and serve others. Hebrews 13:16, (NIV) tells us, *"And do not forget to do good and to share with others, for with such sacrifices God is pleased."*

WHERE TO BEGIN

Have you ever thought, "Why doesn't somebody do something about this?" Well, this may be the nudging of the Holy Spirit for you to take action in that area of need. The Lord gave me a dream to illustrate this point. In this dream, I was in a shoe store and saw many shoes that were my size and style. Shoes represent our sharing the Gospel.[7] The store owner told me to pick out any shoes I'd like. So, I picked a few pairs of shoes and then woke up. Upon waking, I was left with the impression that I could pick from several ministries that fit me, but the point was that I needed to pick something and be faithful to walk it out. It says in 1 John 3:18 (NLT), *"Dear children, let's not merely say that we love each other; let us show the truth by our actions."* God has a purpose and a plan for each of us, and it is so exciting that we get to be part of His plan.

DO NOT DESPISE SMALL BEGINNINGS

If we are faithful in small things, God will entrust us with more and more. *"Unless you are faithful in small matters, you won't be faithful in large ones"* (Luke 16:10, NLT). Jesus gives us a parable in Luke 19:11-27 and in Matthew 25:14-30. In this story, a nobleman who was called away had entrusted his servants with silver (money) to invest while he was gone. After he had become king, he returned home and called the servants to find out what they had each done with the money. The first made ten times the original amount; the second made five times the original amount, and the king said, *"Well done, good and faithful servant!"* The third brought back only the original amount which he had hidden away. *"I was afraid because you are a hard man to deal with."* The king was angry and instructed his servants, *"Take the money from this servant, and give it to the one who earned the most. 'But, master,' they said, 'that servant has enough already!' 'Yes,' the king replied, 'but to those who use well what they are given, even more will be given. But from those who are unfaithful, even what little they have will be taken away'"* (Matthew 25:14-30 NLT).

According to 2 Corinthians 5:10, believers in Christ will be rewarded for using their gifts and fulfilling the callings God has given to each of us. Years ago, I was given a dream where my friends were coming over to get ready for a celebration. They were all beautifully dressed in different gowns with gorgeous colored shoes that matched their dresses perfectly. Jesus tells us in Matthew 16:27 (NIV), *"For the Son of Man is going to come in his Father's glory with his angels, and then He will reward each person according to what he has done."* In my dream, I was very sad because I had nothing to wear. I had not been obedient to the leading of the Holy Spirit and was therefore not prepared to join in on this celebration. As a result of this dream, I was inspired and purposed myself to listen more closely and follow the leading of the Lord.

Each of us will be held accountable for using our gifts and talents wisely. Just as faith is required for salvation, faith is also required to live in His righteousness. Recently, I had a dream that related to the above dream of my picking out shoes which represented me working in someone else's ministry. Now, years later in this new dream, I was trying on a pair of shoes that were too big for me. These shoes represented the ministry God had for me to do personally. The Lord was showing me I needed to spiritually grow into these shoes to make them mine. I needed to pray God would not only equip me for what He wanted me to do but also pray that my faith would grow to believe for what He was now calling me to do.

It is God's desire for us to mature in our faith and become trained about righteousness so we can live as He intends. (Read Hebrews 5:14.) In John 17:4, Jesus tells us that He brought glory to the Father God by completing the work He was given to do. Likewise, our acts of righteousness (our prayerfulness combined with actions of loving obedience) will bring glory to the Father God.

God gave me another dream about the importance of completing our calling. In this dream, I was holding three babies and was filled with tremendous joy. Each of these babies represented a project God had given me. A few months later, I became very busy with life and didn't work on these projects. In a second dream, my babies were hungry and uncared for in the streets. I desperately gathered them, put them on the counter, and went to get help. I finally persuaded someone to come help care for my babies, but when we returned, the babies were gone.

Upon waking, I knew that the Lord was expecting me to complete the work He had given me and not to rely on others to make it happen. If I did not do what He had called me to do, He would give these projects to someone else who would complete them. So, I knew I needed to do what God had given me to do personally. *"Be strong and courageous, and do the work. Do not be afraid or discouraged, for the LORD God, my God, is with you"* (1 Chronicles 28:20a, NIV). Though we may feel unqualified, Psalm 37:23 (AMP) encourages us. *"The steps of a [good and righteous] man are directed and established by the Lord, And He delights in his way [and blesses his path]."* God will show us His will so we can confidently take our steps. The Apostle Paul, in his letter to Archippus, sends this message in Colossians 4:17 (NIV), *"See to it that you complete the work you have received in the Lord."* God is faithful; He will guide us and be with us to help us to complete our tasks.

> *"Those who live only to satisfy their own sinful desires will harvest the consequences of decay and death. But those who live to please the Spirit will harvest everlasting life from the Spirit. So don't get tired of doing what is good. Don't get discouraged and give up, for we will reap a harvest of blessing at the appropriate time."*
> Galatians 6:8-9, NLT

This Scripture is telling us we must not give up or get discouraged. A few years ago, a family member of mine needed meals. This person was living in a group home, but the meals needed to be prepared in a particular way. When I asked the Lord about whether I should prepare these meals, He gave me a dream where I saw that I was servicing two kitchens. When I awoke, I knew it was God's will for me to make meals for my own family and this other family member.

Later, I took on more responsibilities regarding this person's care and became overwhelmed, and the Lord so sweetly said: "I have given you someone to love." This completely changed my perspective and created a desire in me to want to help. I *knew* it was God's will, and He blessed me and gave me peace and joy for doing it!

Sin is most often thought of as what we have done wrong, but it can also be when we don't do what we are supposed to do. The Apostle Paul warns, *"If anyone does not provide for his relatives, and especially for his immediate family, he has denied the faith and is worse than an unbeliever"* (1 Timothy 5:8, NIV). When we pray and then obey as directed, it will bring us great joy to know we are in God's will, even when it is difficult.

LOOK AFTER ORPHANS AND WIDOWS IN THEIR DISTRESS

If you are still not getting a clear word from the Lord as to what you should be doing as a believer, then begin with what the Apostle James said: ***"Religion that God our Father accepts as pure and faultless is this***: *to look after orphans and widows in their distress and to keep oneself from being polluted by the world"* (James 1:27, NIV). Isaiah 1:17 (TLV) instructs, *"Learn to do good, seek justice, relieve the oppressed, defend the orphan, plead for the widow."* It is so simple: just look for people in need and obey as the Lord shows you! Remember, Jesus did what the Father showed Him to do, and He will show us as well. Sometimes, the Lord will ask us to meet a need which may require money and sometimes even time. But again, the Lord will guide us in these matters. Colossians 3:15 (AMP) reads, *"Let the peace of Christ [the inner calm of one who walks daily with Him] be the controlling factor in your hearts [deciding and settling questions that arise]."*

BE NOT POLLUTED BY THIS WORLD

Notice the second half of James 1:27 (NIV), *"Religion that God our Father accepts as pure and faultless is this: to look after orphans and widows in their distress and **to keep oneself from being polluted by the world.**"* The pollution of this world can be many things, but the Lord showed me in my next dream that this can mean checking out of life—to simply exist. In this dream, Jim and I had an opportunity to move into a very nice luxury living complex. We were about to tour the rooms, and I ran into a friend. I asked her if they were going to live there. To my surprise, she said, "No way, we're getting out of here." We parted ways and began our tour. I looked into the first room, and all I saw was a chair and a big-screen TV. Then I looked in the next room, and again, I saw a chair and a big-screen TV. I saw the same thing room after room. I was filled with anxiety because I thought, "I don't want to live like this—I don't want to waste my life in front of a TV." These people were polluting their lives with the pleasures of this world, wasting it in front of a big-screen TV. Like my friend, I couldn't wait to get out of there.

THANKFULLY! GOD GIVES US SOMETHING TO LIVE FOR —HE GIVES US PEOPLE TO LOVE

If we want to live a life full of meaning, excitement, and purpose, then we need to believe in and receive Jesus Christ as Savior and Lord and continue in faith through prayerful obedience as led by the Word of God and with the help of the Holy Spirit. As we do this, we will soon find that living in His righteousness is a life worth living.

CHOOSE TO LIVE A RIGHTEOUS LIFESTYLE AND CHANGE A CITY

We do not know much about Jesus' life between the ages of thirteen and thirty, but Luke 2:52 (NIV) tells us, *"Jesus grew in wisdom and stature, and in favor with God and men."* We are in favor with God because we choose His Son, and we gain favor with people when we choose to live a righteous lifestyle. As a result of our living a righteous lifestyle, the community around us is changed and blessed. *"By the blessing [of the influence] of the upright the city is exalted"* (Proverbs 11:11, AMP).

The Lord gave me the following dream to illustrate how a city may be exalted. In this dream, I saw many circles representing people, all touching each other. As one circle began to spin, it caused all the other circles touching it to spin, resulting in a chain reaction. Hebrews 10:24 (NIV) encourages us, *"Consider how we may spur one another on toward love and good deeds."*

IN BLESSING OTHERS, WE WILL BE BLESSED

1 Timothy 6:18-19 (NIV) commands those who are rich in this present world to *"do good, to be rich in good deeds, and to be generous and willing to share. In this way, they will lay up treasure for themselves as a firm foundation for the coming age, so that they may take hold of the life that is truly life."* To do good has Heavenly rewards, but doing good for others also has many earthly benefits.

Here are just a few Scriptures that show that:

- *"Trust in the Lord and do good. Then you will live safely in the land and prosper"* (Psalm 37:3, NLT).

- *"I know that there is nothing better for men than to be happy and do good while they live"* (Ecclesiastes 3:12, NIV).

Specifically regarding the poor, I found these to be interesting:

- *"He who is kind to the poor lends to the Lord, and He will reward him for what he has done"* (Proverbs 19:17, NIV).

- *"He who gives to the poor will lack nothing, but he who closes his eyes to them receives many curses"* (Proverbs 28:27, NIV).

- *"Blessed are those who have regard for the weak; the LORD delivers them in times of trouble"* (Psalm 41:1, NIV).

Living the life that is truly life and living in happiness and safety, lacking nothing—I think most of us would agree that is priceless!

COMBINE OUR GIFTINGS AND ACTS OF RIGHTEOUSNESS WITH A BOLD CONFESSION OF JESUS CHRIST

The Apostle Paul wrote in 2 Corinthians 9:13 (NIV):

> *"Because of the service by which you have proved yourselves, men will praise God for **the obedience that accompanies your confession of the gospel of Christ**, and for your generosity in sharing with them and with everyone else."*

In the early days of the Church, the Roman Empire (the government) did little to help the poor. The Church was much more involved in caring for those less fortunate. As the church combined their service with a bold confession of

Jesus Christ, many came to believe and receive Jesus as the Christ, the Son of the Living God.

Jesus paid for all sin, whether others choose to take the pardon or not, but people don't know of this great gift from God until they are told. The Apostle Paul in Romans 10:14 (NLT) asks the question, *"But how can they call on Him to save them unless they believe in Him? And how can they believe in Him if they have never heard about Him? And how can they hear about Him unless someone tells them?"*

You may recall that the message of Jesus Christ is called the Gospel, which means "good news."[8] To many people, hearing the gospel message of Jesus Christ is good news, bringing joy and hope of a loving God into their lives. As believers, we get the privilege of bringing the good news of Jesus Christ to others. Paul continues in Romans 10:15 (NLT), *"How beautiful are the feet of messengers who bring good news!"* Remember, shoes (in this case, feet) represent our personal ministry of sharing the Gospel.

Jesus told His disciples, *"Peace be with you! As the Father has sent Me,* **I am sending you***"* John 20:21 (NIV). Today, we are called to help others come into a loving relationship with the Father God through Jesus Christ. The Apostle Paul explained, ***"For Christ's love compels us*** *... that those who live should no longer live for themselves but for him who died for them and was raised again. ... We are therefore Christ's ambassadors, as though God were making his appeal through us. We implore you on Christ's behalf: Be reconciled to God"* (2 Corinthians 5:14-20, NIV).

How can we be Christ's ambassadors/representatives on Earth?

~By operating in our God-given giftings

~By combining our acts of obedience to the Lord, and

148

~By sharing our personal story of Jesus Christ with others.

These are just a few ways we can help others come to know Jesus Christ, and through Him, a loving Father God.

SHARING JESUS CHRIST WITH OTHERS

We have already discussed the first two ways to help others take their sin debt away. Now, let's look at the third way, and that is to share our faith with others. When we realize the sacrifice made for each of us, we will naturally want to share our love story of Jesus Christ with others. The apostles experienced this overwhelming love for Jesus and stated, *"We cannot stop telling about everything we have seen and heard"* (Acts 4:20, NLT). When we come to know Jesus so personally, we won't be able to stop talking about Him, either.

THE CALL TO SHARE OUR FAITH

We see in the Bible that some people were sent out and given clear callings to do so. The Apostle Paul, for example, wrote that he went to Jerusalem because God revealed to him that he should go (Galatians 2:2). On this mission, Paul would be preaching to non-Jewish people. At that time, Gentiles (non-Jews) were considered unclean outsiders. So Paul, a Jewish man who came to believe and receive Jesus, was stepping out of his tradition to preach about Jesus Christ. Even though it may have been uncomfortable for him, Paul chose to obey the call to go where God told him, and he preached, not only to the Jewish people but also to the Gentile people.

Mark 16:15 (TLV) tells us, *"Go into all the world and proclaim the Good News to every creature."* I love the wisdom given by some American missionaries who went to the Middle East for eleven years. One of them said they had to be sure of their calling because they would be taking their children with them. They learned the language and came to know and love the people as their own family. They saw first-hand the enormous sacrifice these people faced as they chose Jesus Christ. In some parts of the world, everything is risked by becoming a Christian. You may be rejected by your family and friends; you may lose your job and even be martyred.

The people these missionaries met understood that though they could lose everything, they would gain the enormous gift of salvation through Jesus Christ. An example can be seen when, in April 2007, three Christians were tortured and killed for their faith in Jesus Christ. The wife of one of the martyred made an immediate public announcement of forgiveness for the men who had just so brutally murdered her husband, stating the words of Jesus Christ, "*They know not what they do.*"[9] This event caused a reaction in their country, and thousands protested against this barbaric act.

Because the risk is so high in some very dangerous parts of the world, these missionaries I met recommend we be certain of our calling. Jesus prepared us by saying, *"He calls His own sheep by name and leads them out ... His sheep follow Him because they know His voice"* (John 10:3b-4, NIV). *"Whoever serves Me must follow Me; and where I am My servant also will be. My Father will honor the one who serves Me"* (John 12:26, NIV). Again, we become sure of our calling through prayer. Whether we minister locally or overseas, we will want to abide and live in His righteousness through prayerful and loving obedience as the Lord leads.

Most of us will not be called to travel around the world to share Jesus Christ with others, but it is more likely that we will be called to share our faith with those around us. In the Book of John, a woman came to know Jesus and went to tell others in her town about Him. This woman said to Jesus, *"Sir, I can see that you are a prophet"* (John 4:19, NIV). *"Then, leaving her water jar, the woman went back to the town and said to the people, 'Come, see a man who told me everything I ever did. Could this be the Christ?' They came out of the town and made their way toward Him. … Many of the Samaritans from that town believed in Him because of the woman's testimony"* (John 4:28-39, NIV). When the Samaritans came to see Jesus and hear His words for themselves, many more became believers. They said to the woman, *"We no longer believe just because of what you said;* **now we have heard for ourselves,** *and we know that this man really is the Savior of the world"* (John 4:42, NIV). The town had the testimony of this one woman, but then they also had their own personal encounter with Jesus and believed and received Him as the Christ, the Son of the Living God.

This is what so many are looking for—a personal encounter with Jesus Christ to help them to believe He is the Savior of the world. I had a dream in which I saw all these cars stopped in the middle of the road because they had run out of gas. It was such a bad situation, I got out of my car to see what was going on. In my dream, I watched as several Muslim women got out of their cars to pray on their knees toward Mecca. (Mecca is considered the holiest city of Islam.) Then, a large woman got out of her car and walked toward me, saying, "We are looking for the Truth."

With an eagerness to know the truth, this woman and the other women with her could activate their spiritual journey by beginning to read the Holy Bible and ask God for a personal encounter with His Son, Jesus Christ. Reading our Bible is like putting gas in our engine. One night, I had a dream where I was in my car pressing on the pedal, but the car was just puttering. I pressed harder, yet the car would not pick up speed. I had run out of gas! I needed to get more of the Word of God in me, along with the power of the Holy Spirit, so I could continue my journey. Likewise, these women looking for truth needed to read the Word of God (specifically the parts about Jesus) so they could understand and be equipped to begin their journey of coming into an intimate relationship with Him, and through Jesus, come to know a loving Father God.

Many years ago, Jesus appeared to a friend of mine in her dream and told her to, "Read the Book." I found this interesting because she was from a different religion, but she was certain it was Jesus who was speaking to her. So, she began to read the Holy Bible, and she started to go to church services, which helped her understand the words of Jesus. As my friend continued in the Word, over time she came into a strong and lasting relationship with Jesus Christ that changed her life forever. I would hear her very often say, "Oh, I love my Lord," and I know she meant it from her heart.

I remember years ago, Jim and I volunteered in the children's ministry at our church. Very quickly, I came to see the impact of divorce and financial troubles in many families. With new eyes, I understood the importance of families coming to know they are dearly loved by God, and when they learn and obey God's plan, they can live out their lives full of hope, meaning, and purpose—as God intends. This hope is found through coming to know Jesus Christ, the Word of God, and the Holy Spirit.

A few months later, I had a dream where I saw boxes of packaged fish with words written on them. Interestingly, fish brings nourishment to the brain and the heart. In my dream, I was impressed to give Bibles to the children's ministry at our church. If these children could get the Word of God before their eyes and in their ears, it would renew their minds and heal their hearts, allowing them to live an abundant and empowered life.

My dear friend Natalie Jones had this same experience when she was a young girl. Natalie was brought up in a broken home, but at the age of ten, she found a book on the shelf that she began to read. This book was *The Egermeier's Bible Story Book*. Natalie came to know Jesus Christ through reading this children's Bible. Her encounter at this young age opened her eyes to see and know Jesus in a personal way. Today, Natalie is a passionate believer in Jesus Christ and was moved by God to launch a Christian Life & Family TV show called *Parent Compass*.[10]

As we grow in our faith, God will equip us to help others also come to know Him. In 1 Peter 3:15 (NIV), it tells us, *"Always be prepared to give an answer to everyone who asks you to give the reason for the hope that you have."* This is the hope we have in Jesus Christ for an abundant and eternal life. The Apostle Paul wrote, *"I give you this charge: Preach the word; be prepared in season and out of season; correct, rebuke and encourage—with great patience and careful instruction"* (2 Timothy 4:1b-2, NIV). We become equipped and prepared to share Jesus by studying the Word of God. With the Word of God and the guidance of the Holy Spirit (John 14:26), we can share our faith with others so they will believe in and receive Jesus Christ and come to know a loving Father God.

We must be alert and look for opportunities to share with others the message of Jesus Christ, as led by the Holy Spirit. I once had a dream where I was told to "tend to my own garden." In our own garden, we can give as much love and attention as needed. We don't have to go far; we can be fruitful right where we are! With the guidance of the Holy Spirit, we can do as Acts 20:28 (NIV) encourages us, *"Keep watch over yourselves and all the flock of which the Holy Spirit has made you overseers."* Though God allows us the joy of helping others, it is God who makes the seed of Jesus Christ grow in the lives of others.

> *"It's not important who does the planting, or who does the watering. What's important is that God makes the seed grow. The one who plants and the one who waters work together with the same purpose. And both will be rewarded for their own hard work."*
> 1 Corinthians 3:7-8, NLT

We must not be discouraged if someone does not receive Jesus immediately when we share the good news gospel of Jesus Christ. Isaiah 55:11 explains that God will accomplish what He desires and achieve His purposes regarding His Word. We can offer someone the opportunity of the hope of Jesus Christ, but it is their choice to believe and receive Jesus Christ for themselves.

Before sharing Jesus Christ with others, we can pray that God will prepare and open their hearts to receive Jesus as the risen Christ, the Son of God. And pray that the veil that causes them not to see all truth would be removed. *"The god of this age [Satan] has blinded the minds of unbelievers, so that they cannot see the light of the gospel of the glory of Christ, who is the image of God. … For God who said, 'Let light shine out of darkness,' made His light shine in our hearts to give us the light of the knowledge of the glory of God in the face of Christ"* (2 Corinthians 4:4 & 6, NIV).

As believers, we can pray that God would give us the divine opportunity and words to share the message of Jesus Christ clearly and effectively. The Apostle Paul wrote, *"And pray for us, too, that God may open a door for our message, so that we may proclaim the mystery of Christ, for which I am in chains. Pray that I may proclaim it clearly, as I should"* (Colossians 4:3-4, NIV). Paul also stated, *"I have become its servant [to minister Christ] by the commission God gave me to present to you the word of God in its fullness"* (Colossians 1:25, NIV).

The Lord showed me the importance of clearly communicating the message of Jesus Christ in its fullness in this next dream. I was with a group of people, and we had to climb up the side of a building on a tall ladder and cross over to another rooftop. I believe this first building represented the kingdom of this world, and the building that we were trying to get to was the Kingdom of God. In my dream, one person went quickly ahead, but she could not cross over because something was blocking her path. Though she kept climbing higher, she still could not cross over. Then the Devil appeared and pointed at fiery stones nearby, so hot they glowed from within. He said to her, "You are one of those burning stones." Filled with panic and fear, she hurried back to where we were and told us what had happened.

In my dream, I said to the woman, "You do not have to be one of those burning stones—you can receive Jesus Christ." She looked at me as if confused and just shook her head from side to side. I was filled with sadness and frustration because she clearly did not understand what I was talking about. Then I awoke from the dream. I believe the Lord was showing me that this woman needed to be given the opportunity to hear the gospel message of Jesus Christ with clarity and in its fullness.

155

JESUS' DEATH ON THE CROSS ALLOWS US TO CROSS OVER

This woman needed to be told her sins were paid for through the blood sacrifice of Jesus Christ on the cross. Any person who chooses to believe in Jesus Christ and receives Him in exchange for the forgiveness of their sins will not be a burning stone having to pay for their sins for all eternity. Through Jesus, we are forgiven of our sin debt, and the barrier is removed. We are reconciled with God and allowed to cross over into eternal life.

According to the disciple Peter, rather than becoming a burning stone, we may become like the Living Stone, Jesus Christ. *"As you come to Him, a living stone rejected by men but chosen by God and precious, you also, like living stones, are being built up as a spiritual house to be a holy priesthood, offering spiritual sacrifices acceptable to God through Jesus Christ"* (1 Peter 2:4-5, NIV).

It says in 1 Peter 2:7-10 that with Jesus Christ as our chief Cornerstone, we are the people of God, and collectively we form the body of Christ. Think of it this way: Jesus Christ is the head of the body, and we, His believers, form His body—the body of Christ. (Read 1 Corinthians 12:27-31.)

The Apostle Paul writes, *"Just as our bodies have many parts and each part has a special function, so it is with Christ's body. We are many parts of one body and we all belong to each other. In his grace, God has given us different gifts for doing certain things well"* (Romans 12:4-6, NLT). A simple illustration of the body of Christ can be seen in a puzzle. Notice the uniqueness of each piece of a puzzle. Each piece is a different color, size, and shape, and each piece fits in its perfect place. No two pieces are the same, yet each piece is of equal value, and *all* pieces are needed to complete the puzzle. (Read 1 Corinthians 12:12-31.)

The Apostle Paul writes to the Ephesians about the body of Christ in Ephesians 4:11-16 (NIV):

"It was He who gave some to be apostles, some to be prophets, some to be evangelists, and some to be pastors and teachers, to prepare God's people for works of service, so that the body of Christ may be **built up until we all reach unity in the faith and in the knowledge of the Son of God and become mature, attaining to the whole measure of the fullness of Christ** *... speaking the truth in love, we will in all things grow up into Him who is the Head, that is, Christ. From Him the whole body, joined and held together by every supporting ligament, grows and builds itself up in love, as each part does its work."*

As each of us, as believers in Jesus Christ, asks and humbly obeys, we will take our place in the body of Christ and will mature and grow into the headship of Christ. We will be *"built together to become a dwelling in which God lives by His Spirit"* (Ephesians 2:22, NIV).

One night, I had a dream of the body of Christ being united and built up with God's Spirit working powerfully through us. In this dream, many people were in a circular church, and we were all seated facing each other. I watched as people started to be elevated from their seats straight upwards at different levels and times. Some were soaring quickly, and others were being raised up slowly. Since we are seated in Heavenly places with Jesus Christ (Ephesians 2:6), these chairs signified our individual position in the body of Christ. I saw those that were being raised up quickly almost fall off their seat. For this reason, each of us must be firmly anchored in our seat.

157

We are told in James 4:10 and 1 Peter 5:6 (NIV), *"Humble yourselves, therefore, under God's mighty hand, that He may lift you up in due time."* Our being elevated and raised up in the spirit realm is contingent upon our being firmly seated with Jesus Christ and allowing the Holy Spirit to operate in us through our choosing to be prayerful (asking of God) and fasted (humbly obedient to the will of God).

THE POWER OF EACH OF US DOING OUR PART

Recall, in Matthew 16:13-19 (NLT) Jesus asks Simon Peter, *"'Who do you say I am?' He replied, 'You are the Messiah, the Son of the living God.'"* Jesus said this was revealed to Peter by the Father in Heaven. Jesus goes on to say that upon this rock (the revelation of Jesus as the Messiah, the Son of the living God), Jesus will build His Church, *"and all the powers of Hell will not conquer it."*

Because Peter received the revelation of who Jesus was, Jesus gave Peter the keys to the kingdom of Heaven. Jesus then continues, *"Whatever you forbid on earth will have been forbidden in heaven, and what you permit on earth will have been permitted in heaven."* That which is *"in heaven,"* is speaking about the Father God's perfect will.

This means that on the revelation of Jesus, believers who form the body of Christ (His Church) will be built together, and our unified efforts will overcome the evils in this world. People can be unified for the good or unified for the bad as this next dream illustrates.

In this dream, I saw an outdoor area filled with primarily men sitting around drinking alcohol. In the center of this area was a large tree. A boy walked by, and one of the men grabbed him and started to molest him in front of everyone. The man did not even try to hide behind the tree to conceal his evil actions. I looked at the faces of those around me; they were just watching, *doing nothing* to stop this man. I panicked and started to scream and point at the man. Then, to my surprise, everyone around me started laughing. I was shocked by this response, and then everyone began to laugh louder and louder. I awoke and remembered thinking these people were so boldly evil; they had no fear of God or His judgment.

> *"Sin lurks deep in the hearts of the wicked, forever urging them on to evil deeds. They have no fear of God to hold them back. Instead, in their conceit, they think they can hide their evil deeds and not get caught. Everything they say is crooked and deceitful; they are no longer wise and good. They lie awake at night to hatch their evil plots instead of planning how to keep away from wrong."*
> Psalm 36:1-4 TLB

This evil man in my dream was clearly guilty, but those who permitted this behavior to continue were now participants and guilty as well. But with each of us being led by the Spirit and doing our part in the body of Christ (His Church), evil cannot prevail.

When we are united, God will do things through us that are greater than we could ever think or imagine. God's power will be expressed mightily and in various ways as we are faithful to operate in our own personal assignments. Jesus tells us, *"Very truly I tell you, whoever believes in Me will do the works I have been doing, and they will do even greater things than these because I am going to the Father. And I will do whatever you ask in My name, so that the Father may be glorified in the Son. You may ask me for anything in My name, and I will do it"* (John 14:12–14, NIV).

As we join forces with God in humble obedience to His will, God will move mightily, as He did through Moses of the Old Testament. Moses lived a righteous lifestyle, being both prayerful and fasted to the obedience of God (Exodus 34:28). Though Moses was not perfect, Numbers 12:3 (NIV) records that *"Moses was a very humble man, more humble than anyone else on the face of the earth."*

Pharaoh, King of Egypt, on the other hand, set himself against Moses and God's people. Pharaoh thought he held the power and was in control, but God showed Himself to be all-powerful. In Exodus 9:16 (TLV), God told Moses to say to Pharaoh, *"I have let you stand for this reason: to show you My power, and that My name might be proclaimed throughout all the earth."* Moses was willing to obey God, and God raised him up above Pharaoh's power and displayed for all the earth to see that God is God Almighty.

How does God display His power on the Earth?

1 Knight and Ray, *Layman's,* 324.

2 G859 - aphesis - *Strong's Greek Lexicon* (kjv) Blue Letter Bible. Accessed Mar 5, 2025 https://www blueletterbible.org/lexicon/g859/kjv/tr/0-1/

3 Gracia Burnham with Dean Merrill, *In the Presence of My Enemies,* (Tyndale House Publishers, Inc., Carol Stream, Illinois 2010).

4 Katie Souza, *Healing Your Soul, "Closing the Door to Sickness!"* Uploaded February 16, 2014, YouTube video, 2:50, http://youtube.com/watch?v=4xVx9X1QPiw, Katie Souza Ministries, https://www.katiesouza.com, Accessed May 22, 2021.

5 Dr. Bruce Wilkinson, *Teach Every Nation,* https://www.Teacheverynation.org; https://www.brucewilkinsoncourses.org. Accessed September 14, 2022.

6 Feed My Starving Children; https://www.fmsc.org. Accessed September 20, 2022.

7 Milligan, *Understanding the Dreams You Dream*, 216.

8 Knight and Ray, *Layman's*, 127.

9 Daniel Blake, "Turkey Christian Missionaries Horrifically Tortured Before Killings," *Christianity Today*, 26 April 2007, https://www.christianitytoday.com/news/turkey-christian-missionaries-horrifically-tortured-before-killings, Accessed March 5, 2025.

10 Natalie Jones, *Parent Compass, Christian Life and Family Show*, https://www.parentcompass.tv, Accessed May 20, 2015.

Chapter Six

GOD IS SO POWERFUL, HE CAN DO ANYTHING! ANYTHING CAN HAPPEN WITH GOD!

There are many accounts in the Bible of God doing the impossible. Luke 1:37 (NKJV) says, *"For with God nothing will be impossible."* In other words, **anything can happen with God.** One of the greatest examples of God's power is demonstrated through Moses's life. Let's examine more closely how God did the impossible and displayed His power on Earth.

In Moses' time, the Hebrew people were slaves to the Egyptians. Moses was born a Hebrew but was taken in and reared by the Egyptian royal family. One day, he came to learn he was a Hebrew, and his eyes were opened to the struggles of the Hebrew people. Shortly thereafter, Moses saw an Egyptian man beating a Hebrew man, and he killed the Egyptian in defense of the Hebrew man. In fear, Moses fled to the wilderness. Years later, God told Moses to go back and lead the Hebrew people out of slavery from Egyptian rule.

Moses obeyed as directed, and God's power was displayed for all to see. Ten plagues fell upon the Egyptians until Pharaoh finally agreed to let the Hebrew people go, and God parted the Red Sea for millions of Hebrews to cross safely (Exodus 7-15). As they journeyed, they were miraculously fed and given water. Interestingly, according to the Bible, not one was sick among the Hebrew people. This was because God's presence was with them, keeping them safe and protected. We see in this account that God worked mightily through Moses. And Moses said to God:

> *"You say to me, 'Bring up this people,' but You have not let me know whom You will send with me. Yet You have said, 'I know you by name, and you have also found grace in My eyes.' Now then, I pray, if I have found grace in Your eyes,* **show me Your ways, so that I may know You,** *so that I might find favor in Your sight. Consider also that this nation is Your people.*
> *'My presence will go with you, and I will give you rest,' He answered. But then he said to Him, 'If Your presence does not go with me, don't let us go up from here! For how would it be known that I or your people have found favor in Your sight? Isn't it because You go with us, that distinguishes us from all the people on the face of the earth?' Adonai answered Moses, 'I will also do what you have said, for you have found favor in My sight, and I know you by name.' Then he said, 'Please, show me Your glory!' So He said, 'I will cause all My goodness to pass before you' . . . ."*
> Exodus 33:12-19a, TLV

God honored Moses' request and was with Moses to guide and help him. Notice that Moses desired to know God and developed an intimate relationship with Him. This intimacy allowed Moses to see God's nature and that God had a love for people. Moses was obedient, and God worked mightily through Moses and displayed His power, showing that **He is so powerful He can do anything! Anything can happen with God!**

Sadly, along the way, Moses' brother and sister, Aaron and Miriam, grew jealous of Moses. *"'Has the Lord spoken only through Moses?' they asked. 'Hasn't He also spoken through us?' And the Lord heard this"* (Numbers 12:2, NIV). It would seem as though Aaron and Miriam wanted God to operate through them—they wanted the power but didn't have the same relationship with God. This made the difference, as Moses took the time and desired to know God's ways and to understand Him more fully. Aaron and Miriam only needed to ask God, as Moses did, to have the same relationship with Him. Recall that Moses asked God in Exodus 33:13 (TLV), *"Now then, I pray, if I have found grace in Your eyes, **show me Your ways, so that I may know You**, so that I might find favor in Your sight."*

JESUS HAD A RELATIONSHIP WITH THE FATHER GOD

The New Testament provides examples of Jesus knowing the Father God intimately. How did Jesus maintain a relationship with the Father God? By spending time with Him.

- *"But Jesus often withdrew to the wilderness for prayer"* (Luke 5:16, NLT).

- *"Very early in the morning, while it was still dark, Jesus got up, left the house and went off to a solitary place, where he prayed"* (Mark 1:35, NIV).

- *"Jesus went up on a mountain to pray, and he prayed to God all night"* (Luke 6:12, NLT).

Jesus nurtured His relationship with the Father God, and one day in the temple, He boldly spoke these words (quoting from Isaiah 61):

165

"The Spirit of the LORD is upon Me,
Because He has anointed Me
To preach the gospel to the poor;
He has sent Me to heal the brokenhearted,
To proclaim liberty to the captives
And recovery of sight to the blind,
To set at liberty those who are oppressed;
To proclaim the acceptable year of the LORD."
Luke 4:18-19, NKJV

When Jesus read these words from Isaiah 61 in the temple, He was speaking about Himself. Because God's anointing presence was with Him, Jesus healed the sick, fed the multitudes, was kind to the dejected, delivered the oppressed, and produced miracles, signs, and wonders on Earth. In Acts 2:22 (KJV), the disciple Peter explains that Jesus was *"approved of God among you by miracles and wonders and signs, which God did by Him in the midst of you."*

Interestingly, Isaiah spoke of the coming of Jesus and said, *"'Behold, the virgin shall be with child, and bear a Son, and they shall call His name Immanuel,'* which is translated as *'**God with us**'"* (Matthew 1:23, NKJV). I had always wondered why He was called Immanuel if His name was Jesus? Jesus was called Immanuel by the people because God was with Him and with Him from the beginning. So now, God was with Jesus on the earth as He did the work of the Lord.

"And you know that God anointed Jesus of
Nazareth with the Holy Spirit and with power.
Then Jesus went around doing good and healing all
who were oppressed by the devil,
for God was with Him."
Acts 10:38, NLT

In the Bible, we read that a man named Nicodemus came to Jesus by night and said to Him, *"Rabbi, we know that You are a teacher come from God; for no one can do these signs that You do unless God is with him"* (John 3:2, NKJV).

GOD'S POWER EXPRESSED THROUGH JESUS

The Apostle Luke records that as Jesus was teaching, *"The power of the Lord was present to heal them"* (Luke 5:17b, NKJV). The Apostle Luke tells us, *"A great number of people from all over Judea, from Jerusalem, and from the coast of Tyre and Sidon, had come to hear Him [Jesus] and to be healed of their diseases. Those troubled by evil spirits were cured, and the people all tried to touch Him because power was coming from Him and healing them all"* (Luke 6:17b-19, NIV).

KNOWING WHO JESUS IS

As Jesus' reputation spread, people began to seek Him out. *"When the men of that place [in Gennesaret]* **had knowledge of Him***, they sent out into all the country round about, and brought unto Him all that were diseased; and besought Him that they might only touch the hem of His garment: and as many as touched were made perfectly whole"* (Matthew 14:35-36, KJV).

In Mark 9:17-25 (NIV), Jesus' disciples could not drive out an evil spirit from a boy. The boy was then brought to Jesus. *"When the spirit saw Jesus, it immediately threw the boy into a convulsion. He fell to the ground and rolled around, foaming at the mouth."* The father of the boy told Jesus that his son had been tormented like this from his childhood. Jesus told the boy's father, *"Everything is possible for one who believes."* (In the Tree of Life Version, verse 23 reads: *"All things are possible for one who believes!"*) The boy's father cried out, ***"I do believe; help me overcome my unbelief!"*** The boy's father wanted to believe

167

and asked Jesus to help him overcome his unbelief. In doing this, he was now putting his faith in the power of God to heal instead of the power of the evil spirit to harm his son. Jesus then told the unclean spirit in the boy, *"I command you, come out of him and never enter him again!"* With these words, the boy was **delivered** from the evil spirit.

There are many examples of Jesus delivering and healing people of sickness and disease in the Bible. A simple way to understand the difference between deliverance and healing can be illustrated by a workman's vise. If your hand is in a workman's vise, that vise is putting pressure on your hand. When you release the pressure of the vise, your hand is set free, and you are delivered. Suppose the pressure was so great that the vise crushed your hand. Not only do you need to be delivered, but you also need to be healed from the injury the vise has caused.

Notice that many people in the Bible received revelation that Jesus was the Son of God because they saw His great love and compassion for them. Jesus, being the good Shepherd that He was, radiated God's love, and this stirred up their faith for the power of God to flow through Jesus to deliver them from evil spirits and to heal them.

For twelve years, a woman in the Bible had an issue of blood in her body, something like hemorrhaging. This woman heard of Jesus and pressed through the crowd to touch the hem of His garment. God's power flowed through Jesus to deliver and heal this woman. The story tells us, *"Immediately her bleeding stopped, and she felt in her body that she was freed from her suffering. At once Jesus realized that power had gone out of Him"* (Mark 5:29-30, NIV). He turned around and asked who it was that touched Him, but no one knew, for it was very crowded.

The woman was identified, and Jesus instructed her, *"Daughter, thy faith hath made thee whole; go in peace, and be whole of thy plague"* (Mark 5:34, KJV). The Tree of Life Version (TLV) reads: *"Daughter, your faith has made you well. Go in shalom [peace] and be healed from your disease."* Jesus is speaking of total and complete healing. This woman's faith in knowing Jesus Christ as the Son of God made her whole. She was spiritually saved (she was made right with God—taking on His righteousness), physically delivered (*"be whole of thy plague"*), healed (*"be healed from your disease"*), and mentally made well (she was freed from her suffering—*"Go in peace"*).

THE HEALING POWER OF JESUS CHRIST

Notice in the above stories that Jesus had not yet gone to the cross—He was operating in the Father God's anointing presence with the Holy Spirit and with power. Matthew 8:17 (NIV) recorded that Jesus' death and resurrection on the cross *"was to fulfill what was spoken through the prophet Isaiah, 'He [Jesus] took up our infirmities and carried our diseases.'"* Isaiah 53:4-5 (TLV), which is speaking of Jesus, reads: *"Surely He has borne our griefs and carried our pains. Yet we esteemed Him stricken, struck by God, and afflicted. But He was pierced because of our transgressions, crushed because of our iniquities. The chastisement for our shalom [peace] was upon Him, and by His stripes we **are healed**."* The word healed is "rapa," (pronounced raw-faw') which means: "to heal, make healthful, physician, cure, repair and make whole."[1]

Jesus went to the cross not only for the forgiveness of our sins but so we may be delivered, healed, and given peace. The Apostle Peter explains in 1 Peter 2:24 (TLV), which is found in the New Testament, *"He Himself bore our sins in His body on the tree [the cross], so that we, removed from sins, might live for*

169

righteousness. 'By His wounds you __were__ healed.'" Healed here is the word "iaomai" which means: "to cure, heal, to make whole, to free from errors and sins, to bring about (one's) salvation."[2] Because Jesus took on our sins, sicknesses, and worries at the cross 2000 years ago, we are offered forgiveness, deliverance, healing, and peace.

When did Jesus give us peace in exchange for our worries? Just before Jesus went to the cross, He went to the Garden of Gethsemane at the foot of the Mount of Olives to pray. At this time, Jesus took on tremendous mental torment. He prayed, *"Father, if You are willing, take this cup from Me; yet not My will, but Yours be done.' An angel from Heaven appeared to Him and strengthened Him. And **being in anguish**, He prayed more earnestly, and His sweat was like drops of blood falling to the ground"* (Luke 22:42-44, NIV). "Anguish" means mental or physical suffering or extreme distress.[3] Jesus was mentally anguished about having to go to the cross. Jesus took on this physical and mental/emotional torment so we might be brought into the restful, peaceful presence of the Father God. On the cross, Jesus not only took away our sins, giving us Salvation, but He took our iniquities and our mental/emotional torment, giving us Peace, and by His wounds, we are delivered and healed.

GOD'S POWER EXPRESSED THROUGH THE APOSTLES OF CHRIST

From the book of Acts through to the book of Revelation, we see the power of God operating through believers in Jesus Christ. Jesus told the disciples to *"go, preach this message: 'The kingdom of heaven is near.' Heal the sick, raise the dead, cleanse those who have leprosy, drive out demons. Freely you have received, freely give"* (Matthew 10:7-8, NIV). After Jesus was taken up to Heaven, the disciples *"went everywhere and preached, and the* **Lord worked with them, confirming what they said by many miraculous signs"** (Mark 16:20, NLT). In Acts 3-4, Peter and John told the people of a beggar who was crippled from birth and had been healed. As a result, the believers raised their voices and prayed in Acts 4:29-31 (NKJV):

> *"... Grant to Your servants that with all boldness they may* **speak Your word, by stretching out Your hand to heal, and that signs and wonders may be done through the name of Your holy Servant Jesus.** *And when they had prayed, the place where they were assembled together was shaken; and* **they were all filled with the Holy Spirit**, and **they spoke the word of God with boldness."**

God honored the prayers of the believers and moved mightily through them. *"God confirmed the message by giving signs and wonders and various miracles and gifts of the Holy Spirit whenever He chose"* (Hebrews 2:4, NLT). These gifts of the Holy Spirit are recorded in 1 Corinthians 12:4-11.

We see God moving mightily when the Apostle Paul prayed for a chief official's father. *"His father was sick in bed, suffering from fever and dysentery. Paul went in to see him and, after prayer, placed his hands on him and healed him. When this had happened, the rest of the sick on the island came and were cured"* (Acts 28:8-9, NIV). This event turned many people's hearts toward God, and they came to believe in and receive Jesus Christ. Paul explains, *"My message and my preaching are not with wise and persuasive words, but with a demonstration of the Spirit's power, so that your faith might not rest on man's wisdom, but on* **God's power"** (1 Corinthians 2:4, NIV).

171

Paul prayed that we *"will understand the incredible **greatness of God's power for us who believe Him**. This is the same mighty power that raised Christ from the dead and seated Him in the place of honor at God's right hand in the heavenly realms. Now He is far above any ruler or authority or power or leader or anything else—not only in this world but also in the world to come"* (Ephesians 1:19-21, NLT).

The Lord gave me the following dream to help me understand the incredible greatness of God's power. In this dream, we were on the top level of an oceanfront hotel room. As I looked out, I saw the ocean water lift up and meet the wind in the sky to form an enormous hurricane (what looked like a water whirlwind). It was huge, and it started to move toward us. When it hit, I fell backward in a gush of water and wind. I asked the Lord, "Is this for our harm or our good?" Then I received the understanding that this huge hurricane symbolized the power of God coming to us through water and wind. When we immerse ourselves in the water **(Word)** and wind **(Spirit)**, the two together will bring the **power of God** into our lives. When this happens, it will always be for our greatest good!

Let's take a quick look at previous chapters regarding the **Word** and the **Spirit**.

> Through Jesus Christ, we are spiritually born into the family of God and have become a new creation in Him. With the righteousness of God in Jesus Christ in us, we are to continue in faith through God's Word. As we continue in God's Word, the Holy Spirit helps us and guides us to all truth. Then, as we come to know and obey the truth, this truth will set us free, and we will begin to live the transformed life that comes from following the Lord.

172

As we abide in and walk with Jesus (through the Word, Spirit, prayer, and obedience to the will of the Father God), we will be coming under His headship and taking our place in the Church, the body of Christ (Ephesians 4:11-16).

In this process, our relationship with Jesus Christ grows and matures, and we come to know Him and the Father God in a very personal way. This creates a desire in us to abide in Him now and forever through praise, worship, and prayer. God's presence, His anointing, allows His power to flow through us so we may live an abundant life and see His mighty hand move on Earth through signs, wonders, and miracles.

In this next dream, the Lord showed me again how we may begin to be guided by the Word and the Spirit. I saw a group of women. These women had never heard the voice of the Lord before, but now they were hearing His voice with definite clarity. Each had their own personal experience with God, and He was specifically directing them in their lives.

Hearing with such clarity will give us the desire to do as God directs, and like Jesus, completing our calling will bring glory to the Father God. All we have to do is start asking in prayer and follow as He directs. With each of us in the body of Christ seeking, listening, and following the Lord's leading, I believe we will see a mighty move of God's Spirit and His power demonstrated on Earth.

But sadly, in the dream above, I saw one woman watching silently. She understood who Jesus was, but she was not open to the ways of the Holy Spirit, so she was purposefully choosing not to participate.

PARTICIPATOR OR ONLOOKER

Remember in Acts 2 after Jesus had ascended to Heaven, those who had gathered were filled with the Holy Spirit, and the people began to praise God in different languages. Onlookers began to hear in their own languages these Holy Spirit-filled people *"declaring the wonders of God"* (Acts 2:11, NIV). The Apostle Peter stood up and explained to the crowd that this was the outpouring of the Holy Spirit as described by the Prophet Joel (Joel 2). In Acts 2, Peter spoke:

"And it shall come to pass in the last days, says God,
That I will pour out of My Spirit on all flesh;
Your sons and your daughters shall prophesy,
Your young men shall see visions,
Your old men shall dream dreams.
And on My menservants and on My maidservants
I will pour out My Spirit in those days;
And they shall prophesy.
I will show wonders in heaven above
And signs in the earth beneath:
Blood and fire and vapor of smoke.
The sun shall be turned into darkness,
And the moon into blood, Before the coming of the
great and awesome day of the LORD.
And it shall come to pass
That whoever calls on the name of the LORD
Shall be saved."
Acts 2:17-21, NKJV

Acts 2 tells us the results of this mighty outpouring of God's Spirit. After Peter told the people about Jesus Christ, those who accepted the message *"were baptized, and about three thousand were added to their number that day"* (Acts 2:41, NIV). This outpouring of the Holy Spirit must have been extremely powerful for so many to receive Jesus as their Savior all at once. It would appear that many onlookers became participants!

The Lord showed me in another dream that we are about to experience another major move of God where many, many people will come to know Jesus Christ. When God's Spirit is poured out on Earth as described in Acts 2, it will be greater than we could ever imagine. In 1939, Smith Wigglesworth prophesied to Dr. Lester Sumrall:

> "I see it—I see revival coming to Planet Earth. I see revival coming to Planet Earth maybe as never before—I see revival coming. It would be untold numbers—untold, uncounted multitudes that will be saved ... So many, so many because nobody will be able to count those that will come to Jesus ... The dead will be raised, the arthritic will be healed, cancer will be healed—no disease will be able to stand before God's people ... It would be a worldwide thrust of God's power and a thrust of God's anointing upon mankind ..."[4]

It's hard to imagine what this outpouring of the Holy Spirit will be like, but one night I had a very exciting dream where I saw the sick healed, people set free and delivered, demons cast out, and many other amazing miracles. In Acts 9:36-42, the Apostle Peter prays for a dead woman named Tabitha, and she opens her eyes, and then he presents her alive. *"This became known all over Joppa, and **many people believed in the Lord"** (Acts 9:42, NIV). Likewise, in my dream, I saw gang members' chains turn to pure gold, meaning that even the most hardened people would be changed and turn to God. A chain around the neck represents a yoke. Where they were once led around by evil, they were now clean, purified, and following the Lord God Almighty.

The above dream continued, and I asked, "Where did they get their teaching that these miracles are happening? Did they get it from Bethel?" Bethel, in the Bible, speaks of open Heavens and blessings being poured out onto the Earth.[5]

In Genesis 28, Jacob, son of Isaac of the Old Testament, was traveling toward Haran. At sundown, *"he found a stone to rest his head against and lay down to sleep. As he slept, he dreamed of a stairway that reached from the earth up to heaven. And he saw the angels of God going up and down the stairway. At the top of the stairway stood the Lord."* God said to him: *"All the families of the earth will be blessed through you and your descendants. What's more, I am with you, and I will protect you wherever you go … I will not leave you until I have finished giving you everything I have promised you."* Then Jacob awoke and said, *"What an awesome place this is! It is none other than the house of God, the very gateway to heaven!"* And Jacob *"named that place Bethel"* (Genesis 28:10-22, NLT).

We read of open Heavens in Luke 3, where Jesus was *"baptized; and while He prayed, the heaven was opened. And the Holy Spirit descended in bodily form like a dove upon Him, and a voice came from heaven which said, 'You are My beloved Son; in You I am well pleased'"* (Luke 3:21-22, NKJV). We see that while Jesus was praying, Heaven opened, and the Holy Spirit came upon Him.

In another dream, I saw that the Heavens will open in this coming mighty move of God, and God's Spirit will be poured out on the Earth. This move of God will be so impactful that it will create a burning desire in people to want to know God and live for Him. I saw people coming to churches hungry for a miraculous touch from God. Though they looked normal to the natural eye, God opened my eyes to see in the spirit realm, and I saw that many people in the church were wearing very exposing, inappropriate clothing. I thought this was so strange! Then as God touched people, I saw unclean spirits begin to exit the Church in a single file. Everyone in the Church was suddenly cleansed of all ungodly spirits and were solemn toward the Lord. The word "solemn" was emphasized, which means deep sincerity. These people were now so impassioned, and they wanted to know what this Jesus thing was all about and how they could be part of it.

In another dream, I saw people coming from far off just to be in God's presence. I saw three (all-day) services being held in an outdoor venue setting which still could not accommodate all the people. There were just so many people wanting to know Jesus. I thought, "Oh Lord, how do we help all these people? There are so many looking to know You and seeking Your healing touch. How can we possibly help all these people?"

To help everyone understand this great move of God on Earth, the Lord explained that our part is to present the Word, the message of Jesus Christ. This is so each and every person who chooses to participate has the opportunity to come to know the **WORD—Jesus Christ**. And it is God's part to *HEAL*—total and complete healing: spiritually, mentally, and physically (Exodus 15:26).

TO KNOW THE WORD—JESUS CHRIST

Here is a quick summary from previous chapters:

Jesus Christ is the Word made flesh, the Living Word, and the written-living Word of God is the Scriptures, the Holy Bible. Jesus died on the cross and

177

was raised from the dead to pay for our sin debt so we may be brought into (right) relationship with the Father God where we may have an abundant and eternal life. When we exchange our sins for belief in Jesus Christ and receive Him, not only are our sins forgiven, but we are offered peace and deliverance, and by His stripes we are healed.

HEALED THROUGH THE POWER AND NAME OF JESUS CHRIST

Many years ago, a young child in our family became very ill with severe diarrhea and quickly became lethargic and dehydrated. The doctors immediately ran tests and determined he had salmonella poisoning. Several days later, there was increased concern when he did not urinate for about twelve hours. We knew his condition was serious, and we began to speak life into his body, specifically life to his kidneys, in the name of Jesus Christ. Moments later, when the nurse came into the room to check his diaper, she said, "He's urinated!" From that point on, he continued to urinate on his own and got better.

I often thought of this healing, and then about two years later, the Lord began to explain to me that the power behind our words created the miracle, and that *power is Jesus Christ*. In Mark 16:17-18 (NKJV), Jesus is speaking and states that in His name, signs will follow those who believe and they will *"lay hands on the sick, and they will recover."*

As mentioned earlier, many gifts of the Holy Spirit are listed in 1 Corinthians 12. You may notice when reading this chapter from your Bible that the gifts of healing are one of these gifts. Like our salvation, these gifts of the Spirit cannot be earned. Further, just as God continues to forgive us for our sins today, He also continues to heal today. I believe this because when I was in high school, I was diagnosed with a thyroid condition. As directed by my doctors, I took my medication consistently for over twenty years. Then, through Scripture and various dreams, the Lord began to open my eyes to see that healing is for today, not just for those in Bible days. One day, my husband and I prayed a simple prayer, and God healed me. Under my doctor's direction, I went in for bloodwork and stopped taking my medication. I have had bloodwork done regularly since that time, and my thyroid results have continued to be normal for what is now over twenty-five years.

It is important for each of us to gain a revelation of all that Jesus did for us on the cross. Not only are we forgiven of our sins, but we are delivered, healed, and given peace through Jesus Christ. In Acts 3, a lame man was begging for money as people were going into the temple. Peter said, *"Silver and gold I do not have, but what I do have I give to you: In the name of Jesus Christ of Nazareth, rise up and walk"* (Acts 3:6, NKJV). Peter wanted to give this man something more valuable than silver or gold; He wanted to share Jesus with him. Then Peter took him by the hand, and *"he helped him up, and instantly the man's feet and ankles became strong. He jumped to his feet and began to walk. Then he went with them into the temple courts, walking and jumping, and praising God"* (Acts 3:8, NIV).

Notice that this was not Jesus speaking but the Apostle Peter, a man. Peter, who believed in and received Jesus, was now sharing his faith in Jesus with this man, who was healed. Peter explained to the crowd, *"By faith in the name of Jesus, this man whom you see and know was made strong. It is Jesus' name and the faith that comes through Him that has completely healed him, as you can all see"* (Acts 3:16, NIV). This lame man believed in and received Jesus and was overwhelmed with joy to be completely healed.

Our part is to share the good news of Jesus, and God's part is to heal. In Acts 4:33 (AMP), it is recorded, *"with great strength and ability and power the apostles delivered their testimony to the resurrection of the Lord Jesus, and great grace (loving-kindness and favor and goodwill) rested richly upon them all."* In Acts 5:15-16 (NIV), God's healing power flowed through the Apostle Peter. *"As a result, people brought the sick into the streets and laid them on beds and mats so that at least Peter's shadow might fall on some of them as he passed by. Crowds gathered also from the towns around Jerusalem, bringing their sick and those tormented by evil spirits, and all of them were healed."* Again, this was not Jesus but Peter, an Apostle and follower of Jesus.

Many years ago, I was in a church setting, and while the pastor was teaching about Jesus Christ, people in the congregation began to be touched by God and healed. This was so exciting to see, and it reminded me of Acts 10, where the Apostle Peter was telling a family about Jesus Christ and, *"The Holy Spirit fell upon all who were listening to the message"* (Acts 10:44, NLT). Later, the Apostle Paul wrote about the importance of understanding all that Jesus did for us on the cross so that we will receive and enjoy the benefits of the Holy Spirit. *"Now we have received, not the spirit of the world, but the Spirit who is from God, that we might know the things that have been freely given to us by God"* (1 Corinthians 2:12, NKJV).

I saw the power of God move mightily in yet another dream! In this dream, people were completely amazed to be touched and healed by God, but then they did not know what to do next. As they were walking out of the church, I overheard them asking, "What now? What do we do now?" Because God was filling them with His Spirit, these people in my dream wanted more of God and were eager and willing to change their lives to live for Him. (Read 2 Corinthians 7:1, and Romans 12:1-2.) The Apostle Paul wrote about this transformation process in Titus 2:12-14 (NIV), *"... live self-controlled, upright and godly lives in this present age, while we wait for the blessed hope—the appearing of the glory of our great God and Savior, Jesus Christ, who gave Himself for us **to redeem us from all wickedness** and **to purify for Himself a people that are His very own, eager to do what is good.**"*

These people in my dream believed in and received Jesus, were filled with the Holy Spirit, and were now eager to live for Him, but they did not know how to live their new life. And this is where **the Church—the body of Christ—** becomes a light reflecting Jesus Christ to the world! As believers, we must prepare ourselves, utilizing our collective giftings to help disciple this great influx of people wanting to know Jesus Christ.

In another dream, I was again in a high-rise building with glass windows on all sides. I was looking out the window watching the waves as they were hitting the shoreline. I was waiting and watching for this huge wave I knew was coming. Like the hurricane in my other dream, this huge tidal wave would be God's Spirit and power being poured out onto Earth. Then, for just a moment, I looked away, and it hit! The wave I had been waiting for hit with such force that water was instantly on all sides of the building. I reached down, grabbed a small case, and started out the door. (The case represents being equipped and ready!)

The Lord showed me that to participate with Him in this mighty move on the Earth, we must prepare ourselves. This is a message for each of us in the Church body of Christ—to prepare and be ready for this mighty move of God. It is hard to imagine, but we get to be vessels of the Lord as He performs signs, wonders, and miracles on Earth. If we choose to participate, God will do what to us is impossible. This will be so exciting! **God is so powerful; He can do anything.**

ANYTHING CAN HAPPEN WITH GOD

For God to do the impossible in and through us, we, like Moses, need to have our own personal relationship with Him. In another dream, I saw someone who was given a coat that looked much like a white doctor's coat. (A coat represents covering, anointing, authority, protection ...)[6] This coat represented their personal relationship with God through Jesus Christ. In the dream, when they put on this coat, they began to be lifted up into the air. (This lifting up represents God doing the impossible.) Then others wanted that coat because they also wanted this same awesome experience, but when they put on the coat, they were not lifted up. Disappointed, they took the coat off and set it aside. The coat had no value to them because they needed to have their own personal relationship with God—their own coat—to be lifted up. Realizing that this coat was only ignited by a personal relationship, the owner quickly went to find it, as he now understood its value. As he put on the coat, he was again lifted up. This time, people tried to hold onto the coat, but he was taken away from them and lifted up onto a rock.

The point of this dream is that we must each have our own personal relationship with God. With Him, He will do through us what we cannot do on our own. In other words, **Anything Can Happen with God!** Psalm 27:5 (NIV) states, *"For in the day of trouble He will keep me safe in His dwelling; He will hide me in the shelter of His sacred tent and set me high upon a* *rock."* God will set us on high and protect us, according to Psalm 91 (NKJV).

> *"He who dwells in the secret place of the Most High*
> *shall abide under the shadow of the Almighty.*
> *I will say of the Lord, 'He is my refuge and my*
> *fortress; My God, in Him I will trust.' . . .*
> **He shall cover you** *with His feathers,*
> *And under His wings you shall take refuge; . . .*
> *Because you have made the Lord, who is my refuge,*
> *Even the Most High, your dwelling place,* **No evil**
> **shall befall you,** *Nor shall any plague come near*
> *your dwelling; For He shall give His angels charge*
> *over you, To keep you in all your ways.*
> *In their hands they shall bear you up, . . .*
> *Because he has set his love upon Me, therefore I will*
> *deliver him;* **I will set him on high, because he**
> **has <u>known</u> My name.** *He shall call upon Me, and*
> *I will answer him; I will be with him in trouble; I will*
> *deliver him and honor him. With long life I will*
> *satisfy him, And show him My salvation."*

To easily understand how we will abide under the shadow of the Almighty where we are kept safe in His dwelling, imagine we are holding tightly to a big umbrella. As we walk in oneness with Jesus, we will be walking in God's perfect will and will be under His covering and protection. In this oneness, we have God's power to draw from to live out the life He has planned and called us to. The Apostle Peter wrote in 2 Peter 1:3-4 (TLV) that *"His divine power has given us everything we need for life and godliness, through the knowledge of Him who called us by His own glory and virtue. Through these things, He has given us His precious and magnificent promises, so that through them you may become partakers of the divine nature, since you have escaped the corruption that evil desires have brought into the world."* And the Apostle Paul wrote to Timothy, *"by the power of God who has saved us and called us to a holy life—not because of anything we have done but because of His own purpose and grace"* (2 Timothy 1:9, NIV).

GOD'S POWER EXPRESSED THROUGH RIGHTEOUSNESS

The Apostle Paul prayed, *"God, **by His power**, will fulfill all our good intentions and faithful deeds"* (2 Thessalonians 1:11, NLT). Through choosing to walk in oneness with Jesus, God's power will be expressed through us, as it was with the apostles, prophets, and disciples who followed Him. Below are steps to show the progression and growth of God's power operating in us as we go from glory to glory.

⇒ Recognize we need God and Repent for our sins.

⇒ Believe and Receive Jesus as the risen Christ, The Son of the Living God. Begin to prayerfully read the Word of God.

⇒ Receive the infilling of the Holy Spirit and begin to be led by the Holy Spirit in all areas of our life.

⇒ Follow Jesus by choosing to live in His Righteousness— humbly pray and lovingly obey.

⇒ God will *anoint* us; His glorious presence in us will break off the yoke of the Devil and his demons.

⇒ Come to know and love Jesus in an ever-increasing measure and show the love of Jesus to others.

⇒ Through praise, worship, and prayer to God, His glorious power will operate through us and out to the world.

As we walk with Jesus and begin to live in His righteousness through the Word of God and by the leading of the Holy Spirit, God's glorious power will operate through us, and we will say, as Jesus said in the temple:

"The Spirit of the LORD is upon Me,
Because He has anointed Me
To preach the gospel to the poor;
He has sent Me to heal the brokenhearted,
To proclaim liberty to the captives
And recovery of sight to the blind,
To set at liberty those who are oppressed;
To proclaim the acceptable year of the LORD."
Luke 4:18-19, NKJV

Remember, in this glorious move of God on the Earth, our part is to preach the gospel of Jesus Christ, the Word. We must share Jesus Christ with others so that everyone can have the opportunity to come to know and love Him. Then, as God moves on the Earth, we will see the sick healed, the oppressed delivered, demons cast out, and many other amazing signs, wonders, and miracles. (Recall these scriptures: Hebrews 2:4, 1 Corinthians 12:4-12. Read Psalm 135:6; Psalm 115:3.)

WHY DOES GOD EXPRESS HIS POWER ON EARTH?

Many people have come to believe in and receive Jesus without the evidence of miracles, signs, and wonders. Still, for some, the demonstration of God's power may serve as an entryway to knowing Jesus Christ. Matthew 15:30-31 (NKJV) states: *"Then great multitudes came to Him, having with them the lame, blind, mute, maimed, and many others; and they laid them down at Jesus' feet, and He healed them. So the multitude marveled when they saw the mute speaking, the maimed made whole, the lame walking, and the blind seeing; and they glorified the God of Israel."*

The Bible tells us Jesus did so many miraculous signs that they could not all be recorded, *"but these have been written so that you may believe [with a deep, abiding trust] that Jesus is the Christ (the Messiah, the Anointed), the Son of God; and that by believing [and trusting in and relying on Him] you may have life in His name"* (John 20:30, AMP). The Father God does these miracles because He wants people to see His goodness and be encouraged to choose His Son, His will, and His ways.

Recently, I had a dream where I heard these words, "The Trumpet is blown, Jesus is coming." Joel 2:1 (NIV) reads, *"Blow the trumpet in Zion; sound the alarm on My holy hill. Let all who live in the land tremble, for the day of the Lord is coming. It is close at hand—"* I was excited to hear this but also concerned. I was concerned because, in my dream, I was telling people, "Jesus is coming! Jesus is coming!" But I was not told when He was coming; I only knew we were to tell everyone that He was coming. I woke up thinking: God is so good. He is giving us time—He wants everyone to have the opportunity to believe in and receive His Son, Jesus Christ.

You may recall from Chapter 2 that we mentioned that Jesus ascended to the Father in Heaven, and He will one day come back for us. Jesus told His disciples:

> *"'And if I go and prepare a place for you,* **I will come back and take you to be with Me that you also may be where I am.** *You know the way to the place where I am going.' Thomas said to Him, 'Lord, we don't know where You are going, so how can we know the way?' Jesus answered,* **'I am the way and the truth and the life. No one comes to the Father except through Me.'"**
> John 14:3-6, NIV

186

Jesus is saying that He is the way, and by following Him, we will know the truth and have life—abundant and eternal life—and He will take us to the Father God (John 14:7, John 17:25-26). This homegoing will be at the Father's designated time. As God determines, Jesus will return and take us to be with Him and the Father God forever. The Apostle Paul wrote in 1 Thessalonians 4:16-17 (NKJV):

> *"For the Lord Himself shall descend from heaven with a shout, with the voice of the archangel, and with the trump of God: and the dead in Christ shall rise first: Then we which are alive and remain shall be caught up together with them in the clouds, to meet the Lord in the air: and so shall we ever be with the Lord."*

AN EVENT NOT TO BE MISSED

The Apostle Paul wrote of our joining Jesus. He says that as a man and wife become one when united in marriage, so will Jesus Christ and His believers, the Church, be united.

> *"For the husband is head of the wife, as also Christ is head of the church; and He is the Savior of the body."*
> Ephesians 5:23, NKJV

Recall that Jesus Christ is the head of the Church, and we, the Church, are His body—called the body of Christ. In a marriage, there is a husband and wife, so also Jesus Christ is the bridegroom, and we, as the body of Christ, are His bride. As in any marriage, the bridegroom wants to be with his bride, and this is the same with Jesus and His believers. Let's look again at what Jesus said in John 17:24-26 (NIV), *"Father, I want those You have given Me to be with Me where I am, and to see*

187

My glory, the glory You have given Me because You loved Me before the creation of the world. Righteous Father, though the world does not know You, I know You, and they know that You have sent Me. I have made You known to them, and will continue to make You known in order that the love You have for Me may be in them and that I Myself may be in them." These are words of intimacy. Jesus wants intimacy with us; when we know Him, we will come to know the Father God—intimately.

Again, we do not know when this will take place. At God's appointed time, Jesus Christ, the bridegroom, will return for the body of Christ, His bride, and the two shall be joined together and united as one. John writes of Jesus' coming in Revelation 19:7-9 (TLV):

> *"Let us rejoice and be glad and give the glory to Him! For the wedding of the Lamb [Jesus] has come, and **His bride has made herself ready**. She was given fine linen to wear, bright and clean! For the fine linen is the righteous deeds of the kedoshim [God's holy people, NLT]. Then the angel tells me, "Write: 'How fortunate are those who have been **invited to the wedding banquet of the Lamb!**'"*

BLESSED ARE THOSE INVITED TO THE WEDDING BANQUET OF THE LAMB

In Matthew 22, Jesus gives us a parable about our joining Him at a wedding banquet. In this parable, a man entered the wedding ceremony feast but did not have the proper wedding clothes and was kicked out. Jesus spoke in a parable, saying:

> *"The kingdom of heaven may be compared to a king who made a wedding feast for his son. He sent out his servants to call those who were invited to the wedding*

feast, but they wouldn't come. Again he sent out other servants, saying, Tell those who were invited, 'Look, I've prepared my meal. My oxen and fattened cattle are killed, and everything is ready. **Come to the wedding feast!'**

But paying no attention, they went away, one to his own farm, another to his business. And the rest grabbed his servants, humiliated them, and killed them. Now the king became furious! Sending his troops, he destroyed those murderers and set fire to their city. Then he said to his servants, 'The wedding feast is ready, but those who were invited were not worthy. So go into the highways and byways, and invite everyone you find to the wedding feast.' And those servants went out into the highways and gathered together all they found, both bad and good; and the wedding was filled with guests.

But when the king came in to look over the guests, he saw a man there who wasn't dressed in wedding clothes. 'Friend,' he said to him, 'how did you get in here without wedding clothes?' But the man was silent. Then the king said to his servants, 'Tie him up hand and foot, and throw him into the outer darkness; in that place will be weeping and gnashing of teeth.' For many are called, but few are chosen."
Matthew 22:2-14, TLV

In this Scripture, a man was kicked out of the wedding feast for not wearing the required wedding clothes. The Prophet Isaiah describes the wedding clothes.

"I will greatly rejoice in the LORD, My soul shall be joyful in my God; **For He has clothed me with the**

189

> *garments of salvation,*
> *He has covered me with the*
> *robe of righteousness,*
> *As a bridegroom decks himself with ornaments,*
> *And as a bride adorns herself with her jewels.*
> *For as the earth brings forth its bud,*
> *As the garden causes the things that are*
> *sown in it to spring forth,*
> *So the Lord GOD will cause righteousness and*
> *praise to spring forth before all the nations."*
> Isaiah 61:10-11, NKJV

In the dream about the required wedding clothes for the wedding feast, the Lord explained that we must wear both the "garments of salvation and the robe of righteousness *to be with Him*." I was confused by this and asked, "Then what does being saved mean?" The Lord said, "You are saved from Hell." (See 1 Corinthians 3:11-15.) Recall, it is by grace through faith that we are saved (Ephesians 2:8-9). The "garments of salvation and the robe of righteousness" are given by God to those who believe in and receive His Son, Jesus Christ. They represent being saved from Hell and brought into a new life in His glorious Kingdom.

Romans 10:10 (TLV) tells us, *"For with the heart it is believed for righteousness, and with the mouth it is confessed for salvation."* To explain this, let's look at the real-life example of Jesus hanging on the cross. Remember in Luke 23:39-43, the criminal hanging next to Jesus was minutes away from death, yet he very quickly came to see and know that Jesus was the Son of God and wholeheartedly put his faith into believing in Jesus. He showed compassion for Jesus and rebuked the other criminal, saying, *"Do you not even fear God, seeing you are under the same condemnation"* (Luke 23:40, NKJV)? Further, he confessed that he deserved punishment for his actions, but that Jesus had done nothing wrong. He said to Jesus, *"Lord, remember me when You come into Your kingdom"* (Luke 23:42, NKJV). And Jesus said to him, *"Assuredly, I say to you, today you will be **with Me** in Paradise."*

Now, switching back to the parable, notice that the King of the wedding feast invited both the bad and the good to attend. Would you say this criminal next to Jesus was an example of bad? He said so himself and admitted he had done wrong and deserved punishment, yet Jesus tells him they will be together in Paradise. Yes, this criminal was bad, but upon believing and receiving Jesus in his heart, he was changed, and in an instant, he became a new creation and was made righteous. Romans 4:7-8 (TLV) tells us: *"Blessed are those whose lawless deeds are forgiven and whose sins are covered. Blessed is the man whose sin Adonai [the Lord] will never count against him."*

What happened that Jesus would bless this man by saying they would be together in Paradise? This criminal believed that Jesus was the Son of God, and he acknowledged that he was a sinner and stated that he wanted to be with Jesus—he received Jesus. **Because he believed and received Jesus in his heart, he confessed it with his mouth** (Romans 10:10). Jesus tells us in Matthew 12:34b (TLV), *"For from the overflow of the heart the mouth speaks."* (Also read: Acts 4:20.) As a result of this man's belief in Jesus, he responded with what was in his heart. Basically, his belief compelled him to react, and his actions and words reflected his pure heart toward Jesus.

This is what Jesus and the Father God want; They want to be in union with people whose hearts are pure toward Them and who know and love Them (Revelation 3:16-17). Remember, it is a wedding ceremony, after all! So, it is understandable that Jesus will want to be with those believers who know Him and love Him.

God loves us and wants a loving relationship with us, and Jesus is our connection to the Father God. If we know and love Jesus, we will know and love the Father God. And this is ultimately what God is after ... He wants our heart.

Though this criminal was admittedly guilty, Jesus saw his changed heart and received him to be with Him for all eternity. We cannot presume to judge the condition of someone else's heart. In 1 Samuel 16:7b (NLT), it tells us that only God can judge the condition of our heart, *"People judge by the outward appearance but the Lord looks at the heart."* In a sermon (called the Beatitudes), Jesus spoke, *"Blessed are the pure in heart; for they will see God"* (Matthew 5:8, NIV). Again, it's a heart issue; God wants our hearts.

Notice, however, that the other criminal hanging next to Jesus did not believe or receive Jesus and was, therefore, not chosen to go with Him. The wedding banquet parable explains why he and the guest at the banquet were not chosen. *"For many are called, but few are chosen"* (Matthew 22:14, TLV). The NIV reads: *"For many are invited, but few are chosen."* Like the man who refused Jesus at the cross and the man in the banquet feast parable, not everyone who is invited will respond to the opportunity to believe in and receive Jesus. But God is so gracious that He invites all—the good and the bad—to a new life in Him through believing in and receiving His Son, Jesus Christ.

Sadly, there will be some who, even with this amazing offer, will say no! Jesus gives us a parable in Luke 16:19-31 about a man who was consumed with the things of this world. When he died, he went to Hell and was in torment. He looked up from Hell and asked Father Abraham for mercy. But it was too late; the man had died and missed his opportunity.

Likewise, we are each faced with this same decision. One night, I dreamt that people were entering a bus to be with Jesus. The people entering the bus had chosen to believe in and receive Jesus Christ and were now taking their seats in Him. But one person did not want to get on the bus. Sadly, in my dream, this person decided to stay behind. Then, at the last minute, he changed his mind and started to climb into the back window. We encouraged him to pull himself in, but suddenly, he let go and threw himself back. I was devastated, but he loved the things of this world too much. He did not know that God's way is always better than our way, and what He has for us now and for all eternity is incomparable to the things of this world. The Apostle John warned us:

> *"Do not love this world nor the things it offers you, for when you love the world, **you do not have the love of the Father in you.** For the world offers only a craving for physical pleasure, a craving for everything we see, and pride in our achievements and possessions. These are not from the Father, but are from this world. And this world is fading away, along with everything that people crave. But anyone who does what pleases God will live forever."*
> 1 John 2:15-17, NLT

We can't let the pleasures of this world be a temptation and distract us from choosing Jesus. If we are still alive, it's NOT too late! Like the criminal hanging on the cross next to Jesus who came to believe in Jesus and know Him as Lord just moments before his death, we can believe in and receive Jesus Christ as our Savior and the Lord of our life at any time —even if we are at the very end of our life. As quickly as Jesus received this criminal, so will He also receive us at any stage in life.

As with any loving marriage, both parties willingly receive each other, and the two will be united in Holy Matrimony. This is the goal Jesus, and the Father God have for us—to have intimacy and oneness in a holy relationship. Many years ago, I had a dream where I saw three young girls talking among themselves.

One young girl said, "I want to be closer to God."

The others said, "Yeah, me too." They were believers in Jesus Christ who desired to know God in a greater way, but they didn't know how to get closer to Him. Then I heard the same answer I had heard so many times before, "You can … just spend time with Him through the Word and prayer." The Apostle Paul tells us that all God created can be *"made holy **by the word of God and prayer"*** (1 Timothy 4:4-5, ESV).

SPEND TIME IN THE WORD AND PRAYER

By spending time in the written, living Word of God (the Bible) and prayer, our minds are renewed as the Holy Spirit gives us insights, understanding, revelation, and wisdom. Soon, as we continue to follow Jesus and learn from Him, we will mature in our faith, grow in love, and come to know Him passionately, personally, and intimately. In knowing Jesus, our lives will be transformed and refined, and we will come to know and love the Father God and get closer and closer to Him (John 14:7). Really, isn't this the way we come to know anyone? We spend time with them and choose to be with them, prioritizing them in our lives.

In Jeremiah 29, God says to call on Him and pray to Him, and He will listen. God says in verse 13 (NIV), *"You will seek Me and find Me, when you will search for Me with all your heart. Then I will be found by you."* In 1 John 2:27b-29 (NIV), we are told how we may achieve this closeness:

194

*"… But as His anointing teaches you about all things and as that anointing is real, not counterfeit—just as it has taught you, **remain in Him**. And now, dear children, **continue in Him**, so that **when He appears we may be confident and unashamed before Him at His coming**. If you know that He is righteous, you know that everyone who does what is right has been born of Him."*

As believers, when we remain and continue in Jesus Christ, we will come to know Him, and true relationship and intimacy will be created. We will fall deeply in love with Him. Again, it is in knowing and loving Jesus that we will come to know and love the Father God. And we have only to ask as Moses asked of God, *"**Show me Your way that I might know You**"* (Exodus 33:13, NKJV). I love Psalm 143:8-10 (TLV), which reads as follows:

*"**Make me hear** Your lovingkindness in the morning, for in You I trust.*
***Show me the way I should go**, for to You I lift up my soul.*
***Deliver me** from my enemies, Adonai [Hebrew name for God], I hide myself in You.*
***Teach me** to do Your will, for You are my God.*
*Let Your good Ruach [Spirit] **lead me** on level ground."*
Psalm 143:8-10, TLV

GOD WILL SHOW US THE WAY

One night, the Lord gave me a dream. In this dream, Jim and I were beside a river, and the Lord said, "I am laying down the Jordan; I will be in front of you and behind you."

(Read Psalm 121:8.) God was setting before us an opportunity—He was laying it down for us, but it was up to us to walk it out.

In the Old Testament, God delivered the Israelites from the hands of the Egyptians by allowing the Israelites to cross the *Red Sea*. This was the first crossing the Israelites had to make. Later, the Israelites crossed the *Jordan River* when entering the land God had promised them, and this was the second crossing. Now in my dream, the Lord was setting before Jim and me the opportunity to not only believe and receive Jesus, but to also take that next step of living in His righteousness.

This is what the angel told Joshua about the Israelites crossing the *Jordan River:*

> *"After the death of Moses the servant of the LORD, the LORD said to Joshua son of Nun, Moses' aide: 'Moses my servant is dead. Now then, you and all these people, **get ready to cross the Jordan River** into the land I am about to give to them—to the Israelites. I will give you every place where you set your foot, as I promised Moses. . . . No one will be able to stand up against you all the days of your life. As I was with Moses, so I will be with you; I will never leave you nor forsake you. Be strong and courageous, because you will lead these people to inherit the land I swore to their forefathers to give them. Be strong and very courageous. Be careful to obey all the law my servant Moses gave you; do not turn from it to the right or to the left, that you may be successful wherever you go. Do not let this Book of the Law depart from your mouth; meditate on it day and night, so that you may be careful to do everything written in it. Then you will be prosperous and successful. Have I not*

*commanded you? Be strong and courageous. Do not be
terrified; do not be discouraged, for the LORD
your God will be with you wherever you go."*
Joshua 1:1-9, NIV

The Israelites were promised this land but had to cross
the Jordan River to receive all God had for them. Notice that
both the Red Sea and the Jordan River were steps of faith.

For each of us, the steps of faith are:

> *Crossing The Red Sea*—which symbolizes our repenting
> of our sins and believing in and receiving Jesus as the
> risen Christ, the Son of God.

> *Crossing The Jordan River*—which symbolizes our being
> in oneness with King Jesus through the Word of God
> and following the leading of the Holy Spirit. In this,
> intimacy is created, and we come to know and love
> Jesus; through Jesus, we will come to know and love
> the Father God.

God is laying down the Red Sea and the Jordan River for
each of us. As we cross over, He will be with us every step of
the way (Philippians 1:6, NKJV). For me, recognizing that I
needed to be forgiven of all my sins and believe in and
receive Jesus Christ was the greatest decision in my life. Then,
when I began to walk with Jesus Christ by prayerfully being in
the Word of God and following the leading of the Holy
Spirit, my life began to change. As I continued to remain and
abide in Him, I came to know Jesus and the Father God
personally and in a meaningful way.

And this is how we get closer to God. In a dream, the
Lord showed me I could have more of Him, and I said, "I
didn't know I could have it all." This is having ***all the fullness***

of God, where we can share in the blessings, promises, and benefits of God now on Earth. Psalm 103:2-5 (NIV) reads:

"Praise the Lord, O my soul, and forget not
all His benefits.
Who forgives all your sins
Who heals all your diseases
Who redeems your life from the pit [destruction]
Who crowns you with love and compassion
Who satisfies your desires with good things
so that your youth is renewed like the eagle's."

In Christ Jesus, WE CAN HAVE IT ALL.

"Since, then, you have been raised with Christ, set your hearts on things above, where Christ is seated at the right hand of God. Set your minds on things above, not on earthly things. For you died, and your life is now hidden with Christ in God.
When Christ, who is your life, appears, then you also will appear with Him in glory.

Put to death, therefore, whatever belongs to your earthly nature ... and ... **put on the new self, which is being renewed in knowledge in the image of our Creator.**
Here there is no Greek or Jew, circumcised or uncircumcised, barbarian, Scythian, slave or free, but **Christ is all, and is in all."**
Colossians 3:1-11, NIV

I leave you with one final dream. In this dream, I was asked two questions which we can each ask ourselves:

~ Do you believe in your heart and receive Jesus Christ as your Savior?

~ Is He living and dwelling in you so that you may come to know Him as Lord of your life?

I hope you will say **YES** to the invitation to join the wedding banquet feast of the Lamb. To receive Jesus as your Savior and Lord, pray this prayer:

Dear Heavenly Father God,

I recognize that I need Your love, Your peace, and Your forgiveness. I confess that I have sinned, and I ask that You forgive me. Thank You, Father, for sending Your Son, Jesus Christ, to die on the cross so that I may be forgiven of my sins and brought into a right relationship with You. Lord, I am calling on You now, and I ask that You reveal Jesus to me so that I may know Him and You in a personal way. I believe Jesus is Lord, and I believe in my heart that He died for me on the cross and that He was raised from the dead. I receive Him now so He will live in me and I in Him forevermore. Thank You, Lord, for saving me from the kingdom of darkness and for receiving me into Your glorious Kingdom.

AND THIS IS WHAT THIS JESUS THING IS ALL ABOUT!

THE END

1 H7495 - rapa -*Strong's Hebrew Lexicon* (kjv) Blue Letter Bible. Accessed Mar 5, 2025. https://www.Blueletterbible.org/lexicon/h7495/kjv/wlc/0-1/

2 G2390 - iaomai - *Strong's Greek Lexicon* (kjv) Blue Letter Bible. Accessed 5 Mar, 2025. https://www.Blueletterbible.org/lexicon/g2390/kjv/tr/0-1/

3 G74 - agonia - *Strong's Greek Lexicon* (kjv) Blue Letter Bible. Accessed 5 Mar 2025. https://www.Blueletterbible.org/lexicon/g74/kjv/tr/0-1/

4 Lester Sumrall, *"Lester Sumrall My Relationship with Smith Wigglesworth,"* Transcribed from Raymond Perez's YouTube Channel, Uploaded January 22, 2018, YouTube video, 24:00-25:27, https://www.youtube.com/watch?v=F2NTZyQhuiM.

5 Bill Johnson, *Hosting the Presence: Unveiling Heaven's Agenda,* (Shippensburg, PA: Destiny Image Publishers, Inc., 2012) 89-90.

6 Milligan, *Understanding the Dreams You Dream,* 148.

A Word About Dream
Interpretation

By Shelle Thomas

We read of dreams and visions and their interpretation in the Book of Daniel. In Daniel 2, the king was given a frightful dream and wanted to know the meaning. No one was able to give the interpretation. But **Daniel prayed, and that night, the king's dream was revealed to Daniel in a vision**. Daniel was then able to tell the king not only what his dream was but also the interpretation of the dream. The king was pleased, and the lives of Daniel and his friends were spared. Then Daniel said: *"Blessed be the name of God forever and ever, for wisdom and might are His ... He reveals deep and secret things; He knows what is in the darkness, and light dwells with Him. I thank You and praise You, O God of my fathers; You have given me wisdom and might, and have now made known to me what we asked of You, for You have made known to us the king's demand"* (Daniel 2:20, 22-23, NKJV). **Notice, Daniel prayed and God gave the interpretation of the king's dream to Daniel.**

In the forty-five years I have known Lynn, she has been given dreams from God. Sometimes the dreams were basic and had an obvious interpretation. There were times, however, when the dream was not clear, and Lynn would share with me her dream, and the Lord would give me the interpretation. This would be something like what Daniel experienced in the above story.

If you are given a dream but are not given the interpretation, you can also reference dream interpretation books which can help with the basic meaning and direction.

Some of these books may include *Understanding the Dreams you Dream*, by Ira Milligan and *Dreams & Visions: Understanding and Interpreting God's Message to You*, by Jane Hamon. But with every God-given dream, you will want to pray for the interpretation to understand the meaning for yourself just as Daniel of the Bible did.

To learn more, please contact:

Ira Milligan at https://iramilligan.com

Jane Hamon at https://janehamon.com

I believe the dreams and visions in this book will speak to people and bring life, truth, hope, and salvation. May God bless you as you begin your journey in drawing closer to God through His Son, Jesus Christ. Amen!

ACKNOWLEDGMENTS

I want to thank my sweet Aunt Ellen for all her hard work and years of patient endurance in the writing of this book. The Lord had given me a dream to ask my Aunt Ellen for her help, and I had no idea of the wisdom, knowledge, and understanding she had of the Bible. God directed me to the perfect person to complete this book as we began our journey in 1996!

I also want to thank my husband, Jim, for his support and our son, Daniel, who was so helpful in the structure, editing, and scriptural clarification of this book. And to my amazing friends: Deborah Bailey for scriptural content and editing the book, Shelle Thomas for dream interpretation, and so many others who helped me pray through and gain an understanding of the many dreams and visions in this book. God is so good to place you all in my life. I am truly grateful.

REFERENCES

Mel Bond
F. F. Bosworth
John Connor
Charles and Frances Hunter
Bill Johnson
Joyce Meyer
Ira Milligan
T. L. Osborn
Oral Roberts
Smith Wigglesworth
Andrew Wommack

www.ingramcontent.com/pod-product-compliance
Lightning Source LLC
Chambersburg PA
CBHW061738120626

46550CB00005B/1821